Hands-On Guide to GDPR Compliance

Privacy by Design, Privacy by Default

Karen Lawrence Öqvist

Filip Johnssén

Contents

Chapter 4: The Privacy Program

Chapter 5: GDPR Operational Efficiencies

Foreword

Karen Lawrence Öqvist

"Where and how to start?" That was the first question burning on the lips of every CxO[1] of not only those companies based within the EU, but also any company trading with an EU-based company or EU customers, following the 2016 adoption of the General Data Protection Regulation, or GDPR. Next came a cry for help: "What have we done right—or wrong? And someone please help!" In response, the fall of 2017 brought an array of product and service vendors claiming to have the "magic bullet." But in reality, many were security and risk products/services repackaged as applying to GDPR.

When it comes to legislation that has data protection and privacy at its core, complexity has triumphed over simplicity and laziness has trumped awareness. As a result, there has been a lack of compliance and adoption on the rights of the data subject.

Despite the imperfections that you will hear concerning the GDPR, one thing is for sure: It is better than what we had before. Fundamentally, it attempts to achieve two conflicting goals:

- Facilitate the flow of personal data across national jurisdictions within the EU—after all, Gross National Product (GNP) is important for the growth of us all!

- Protect the privacy of EU data subjects, a goal that stems from the 1953 European Convention on Human Rights.

What strikes me foremost within the legal text of the GDPR, which I really don't like, are the exemptions when it comes to sharing personal data in the name of "national security" and "law enforcement."[2]

---

1   A collective reference to C-level corporate executives.
2   The exchange of personal data within the context of law enforcement is regulated in the directive (EU) 2016/680 of the European Parliament and of the Council of 27 April 2016 on the protection of natural persons with regard to the processing of personal data by competent authorities for the purposes of the prevention,

Moreover, there is the rather sneaky clause concerning "legitimate interest" (Article 6(f)). We'll talk more about these issues later in the book!

However, as a whole, the GDPR tries to fix what was broken before, and more. It attempts to update laws that were outdated and not aligned with today's digital and connected society. It succeeds where other attempts have failed. And in the future, it will fall short, too. After all, technology evolves rapidly, and tried and tested legislation takes much longer to craft and implement. But we must focus on what we have in place and what we know today, not on the unknowns.

Up until recently, issues pertaining to compliance with national data protection laws have been addressed by legal consulting companies or the legal arm of an organization. Yet the Internet of Things (IoT) is the Joker in the pack of cards for the legal profession. IoT is collecting heaps of personal data on each of us. The GDPR is a response to the IoT; to the technology that tracks our choices and our movements, both in the physical and digital worlds, which are now overlapping, the boundaries impossible to separate. We have, each of us, become enmeshed in a digital society.

The GDPR is a new breed of animal graced with a rather impressive set of teeth. Should a data controller show that they are not fit custodians of personal data by losing or otherwise exposing such data, the entity can be fined up to four percent of its annual revenue for each data loss—in addition to the potential damages that can be awarded to the data subject. In other words, this rather "hot potato" has landed at the board level of any international or company operating within the EU. This is not just controllers, it is also the processor who doesn't want to be held liable for the mistakes of the controller. They need to limit the scope of accountability. In many cases, this "hot potato" is too hot for the board, and in turn has been delegated to either the CIO or the compliance arm of the organization. On the surface, this might seem to be a good thing, except many experts are unaware that compliance with the GDPR is not the same as compliance with

---

investigation, detection or prosecution of criminal offences or the execution of criminal penalties, and on the free movement of such data.

Sarbanes-Oxley[3], Basel III[4], PCI-DSS[5], or any infosec program using ISO 27002 as its control framework. GDPR compliance is not a tick-box exercise!

Confusion has come about because these programs, namely the ISO 27002 control framework, has a specific section on compliance with data protection laws. This has resulted in infosec professionals attempting to map privacy compliance into security compliance. That's the wrong approach. And that's why I wrote this book: to explain in a simple way how to deal with compliance with the GDPR.

I am not a legal guy, I am an information security guy (or girl, as the case may be). I have over the years become a geek in IT, digital identity, information security, compliance, privacy, business, management change, and entrepreneurship. I believe that to get this right, we need to do better than we have in the past with information security, which was in all honesty a journey of compromises.

I have been partially inspired by David Lacey, the founder of the Jericho Forum and the brains behind BS7799, which later evolved into ISO 27001. He had and still has a capability to find simplicity within complexity. He has provided me with inspiration to strive for the same level of simplicity in everything I do.

I found additional inspiration in the work of Fred Piper, founder director of the Information Security Group (ISG), and professor at the Royal Holloway University of London (RHUL). He is so highly respected and he explains complicated subjects in such a simple way you wonder really if they really are so complex.

Also influential was a book[6] by Margaret Wheatley, who linked management practices with physics and nature and showed how order and structure underlay the chaos and complexity of the natural world—a lesson that can be applied to organizational thinking.

Finally, there is the International Association of Privacy Professionals (IAPP). It was during my first IAPP Global Privacy Summit in Washington, D.C., in 2015 that I heard the keynote Glenn Greenwald talking about whistleblower Edward Snowden and the responsibility of digital privacy officers in the modern age. It was

---

3   See http://www.soxlaw.com/
4   See https://www.bis.org/bcbs/basel3.htm
5   See http://www.theukcardsassociation.org.uk/security/What_is_PCI%20DSS.asp
6   Leadership and the New Science: Discovering Order in a Chaotic World

immensely inspiring. Following this I became certified in CIPP/E, CIPT, and CIPM. I also discovered the Organization for Economic Co-operation and Development privacy principles, which I consider to be the lowest common denominator in privacy globally.

These four influences have driven my thinking for at least the last 10 years, and also how I have approached writing this book. A final inspiration was Filip Johnssén, who agreed to co-author this book with me. He is a legal geek, philosopher, and comedian, and someone who I am privileged to have as my sounding board and friend over the last two years.

Filip Johnssén

With the release of this book I celebrate a decade of working exclusively with data protection, or as I prefer to call it, "data privacy." To me "data protection" sounds almost like "information security." Not that there's anything wrong with information security, but that term tends to diminish what the field is all about. The origin of data protection can be found in the field of human rights, not IT. It's about the protection of each of us in our capacity as living human beings. We all have an inherent right to privacy. The size and limits of the the private sphere are perhaps still open for discussion, but almost everyone agrees it exists to a larger or smaller extent.

A subset of privacy is data privacy. As the digitized world continues to grow and evolve, this realm gets increasingly important. As we are still at the beginning of this trajectory, it is hard to forecast how data privacy will evolve in a few decades. But what we do know is what the legal framework in the EU looks like from May 25, 2018—it looks like the GDPR. And as with all data protection legislation, it is thereafter all about the implementation. And that is what we have in focus in this book. As far as possible we have tried to exclude complicated legal lingo or deep dives into legal subtlety.

However, I will here and now discuss some of the more philosophical aspects of GDPR. First of all, I can't get away from the feeling that most debaters seem to think the GDPR is something new that just fell down from the sky, or that we started arguing these issues in 2012. Nothing could be more wrong. The concept of privacy has been around as long as mankind; one can find mention in written texts dating back to Aristotle

(4th-century BC), Risalat al-Huquq[7] (Second half of 600), the Magna Carta (1215), and later the European Convention on Human Rights[8] (1953).

Meanwhile, an interesting conundrum is that when privacy is explicitly mentioned it is never defined. Quite often I ask myself if it's even possible to agree on a definition. My conclusion stays the same: No, it's not. It is through this lens that I understand privacy laws and their implications as well as why they look as they do. The GDPR is not an exception. The ultimate question, then, becomes: Is it possible to legislate about privacy? Were the politicians in Brussels correct to adopt a regulation applicable throughout EU? To me this is still an open question and only time will tell.

Don't misunderstand me. I do like the idea of having one general data protection legislation cover the whole of the EU, but I don't know if it will work. Privacy is not a cucumber. We all remember the debate that followed the EU stating how a cucumber should look.[9] Now the EU has tried to state how big the privacy sphere is. But unlike a cucumber, privacy is not measured in centimeters or kilograms. It is an individual experience. What is OK in one situation is not OK in another. Yes, private life needs to be safeguarded, no question about it. But should it be safeguarded in the same way regardless of the contextual, social or historical background? In some sense this goes back to the ongoing debate about legal positivism[10] versus natural law.[11] Even though this is germane to discussions about the GDPR, this political science is not what we will focus on in this book.

For now, let's just accept the GDPR as it is, pros and cons, and try our best to implement it in an easy way. In this book I, together with my very good friend Karen Lawrence Öqvist, will share anecdotes and tips for implementing legal data privacy requirements in a smooth and

---

7   Treaties on Rights.
8   The European Convention for the Protection of Human Rights and Fundamental Freedoms (ECHR).
9   http://www.telegraph.co.uk/news/worldnews/europe/2453204/Bent-banana-and-curved-cucumber-rules-dropped-by-EU.html (Downloaded, April 29, 2017)
10 Legal Positivism is the notion that the law reflects the society and the social order as well as the structure of governance. The law is not measured on its own merits, but its role in society.
11 Natural law is the belief that there are some rights common to all humans in their capacity as humans and that these are not derived from the society and its norms.

effective way. I am very fortunate to have Karen as a friend and co-writer. Whenever I have lost myself in philosophic reasoning, she has pulled me back on track.

I should also state I don't share Karen's view that surveillance is necessarily something bad. Maybe my five years in the Swedish Security Service indoctrinated me to think otherwise. Cameras and wiretapping are not the devil's tools. They are in the public interest.

Who Should Read This Book?

This book takes GDPR compliance straight from the field.

It is an operational book, although we delve into big-picture privacy and GDPR questions and topics in order to migrate you into a "privacy" and "legal" mindset. We have tried to keep the "legal speak" to a minimum, but frankly there is no way you will get into a seasoned role as a GDPR practitioner without some exposure to the legal thinking behind the text.

If you are an IT, security, and/or compliance practitioner who has been tasked with GDPR compliance, then this book is definitely for you. It will extend your skillset into privacy and GDPR.

This book is *not* a comprehensive GDPR legal guide. If you are a legal professional, this book will broaden your knowledge about how to take a legal instrument and convert into an implementation tool. But if you are looking for a pure GDPR legal focus, this book is *not* for you.

Introduction[1]

The GDPR party

After a slow start, things accelerated during 2017, organizations woke up from their coma, and most had a budget to roll out their GDPR projects. (Those that didn't are in a state of panic!)

A common mistake is for organizations to use the GDPR per se as the toolbox to implement compliance across their organization. Earlier we mentioned that the GDPR is a piece of legal art. Hence, it is not a toolbox. It does not explain how to implement. It states you need to have data protection by design as the default mode of operations across your business, but it does not say precisely how to achieve that goal.

We heard over and over that one cannot take a "tick-box approach" to GDPR compliance. So here we have a legal piece of art, that is not styled to execution. Those who have tried have ended up in a GDPR quicksand, saddled with a humongous project, sucking up resources with no end in sight. The legal team is quoting the GDPR principles, while the IT and security guys still think you can treat personal data the same as intellectual property (IP). Regardless, both camps appear to neither understand the basics nor to have consensus on how to approach GDPR.

GDPR product vendors are claiming they can make your organization GDPR compliant, simply with a magic bullet. Unfortunately, many of these "snake oil" offerings are merely security products repackaged as privacy products. The IT and compliance team are easy targets because they may not understand the complexity of the GDPR as well as the data protection legal team does. After a trillion breakfast seminars—mainly sponsored by companies wanting to sell them products and services— the IT, security, and compliance guys are like the blind leading the blind. In short, "snake oil" is a hot commodity on the GDPR market in 2017 and that is likely to be the case until at least 2020!

---

1 All GDPR quotes/extracts are © European Union, http://eur-lex.europa.eu/, 1998-2016

Often, the legal team understands the complexity, but doesn't know how to implement across the business. There are exceptions, and that is where the legal department happens to support a business wherein personal data is the core product, like in the insurance sector. However, the majority of legal professionals have problems communicating with the compliance/IT guys. If GDPR compliance is run by IT there is a trend to conduct privacy risk assessments on IT systems.

Then there's the business executives, who are standing back, expecting this to sort itself out before they get called in to the party. This is a big problem because in order to get data protection by design as a default you need to start with the business functions, and see that you have documented the business processes and assigned ownership. Getting everyone on the same page is the foundation to effectively assessing privacy risk across your organization along with getting an GDPR accountability structure in place.

The DPO shortage

In 2017 the market for the Data Protection Officer (DPO) role in the organization is forecast at circa €6 billon following May 25, 2018. This position is a requirement for many large organizations, especially those which deal with sensitive data, and particularly if that is the core product of a business. Even if an organization does not have, or need, someone in this role full-time, companies will have to incorporate this expertise somehow on their GDPR journey to compliance.

Pick the low-hanging fruit

Many organizations have started on their GDPR journey, and risks are surfacing to expose gaps that point to opportunities to do what should have been done previously.

But you don't need GDPR experts to do all your work. They are after all in short supply and there are a lot out there selling "snake oil." You can get the ITIL/ITSM experts in to fix your IT processes; for business processes, get the black belt in Six Sigma; and for security the infosec guys. Follow industry standards, get the rules in place, document, evidence and find yourself in a nice place when you can focus on personal data.

CHAPTER 1

Privacy Foundations

What is privacy and why is it important?

Privacy *per se* first hit the press big time in 1890 when a paper, "The Right to Privacy," was published by the Harvard Law Review. It turned out to be "one of the most influential essays in the history of American law"[1] and is widely regarded as the first publication in the United States to advocate a right to privacy. It interprets that right primarily as a "right to be left alone." The paper was written by Louis Brandeis and Samuel Warren. Brandeis was an American lawyer and associate justice on the Supreme Court of the United States from 1916 to 1939, and he later acknowledged that the idea for the essay came from Warren's "deep-seated abhorrence of the invasions of social privacy."[2]

> **Article 12 Universal Declaration of Human Rights**
> *No one shall be subjected to arbitrary interference with his privacy, family, home or correspondence, nor to attacks upon his honour and reputation. Everyone has the right to the protection of the law against such interference or attacks.*

---

1 Gallagher, Susan E. "Introduction". "The Right to Privacy" by Louis D. Brandeis and Samuel Warren: A Digital Critical Edition. University of Massachusetts Press.
2 Amy Gajda (2007), What If Samuel D. Warren Hadn't Married A Senator's Daughter?: Uncovering The Press Coverage That Led To "The Right to Privacy". Illinois Public Law and Legal Theory Research Papers Series p. 7,

Since 1890, the base assumption of the right to personal privacy has been recognized around the world in diverse regions and cultures. The Universal Declaration of Human Rights,[3] adopted by the United Nations General Assembly in 1948, includes a right to privacy in Article 12. This was adopted by the European Convention on Human Rights (ECHR) in 1953. Nearly every country in the world includes a right to privacy in its constitution, and if it is not defined explicitly, it is generally acknowledged implicitly as a right.

Privacy is an inherent concept for humanity, yet it presents many dilemmas in society. A particular conundrum is that ideally, we each want privacy for ourselves, yet we would like everyone else to be transparent. This makes absolute privacy per se a difficult feat for any society.

> *'Whenever a conflict arises between privacy and accountability, people demand the former for themselves and the latter for everyone else.'*

> —*David Brin, The Transparent Society, 1998*

This dilemma and more are tackled in the form of privacy laws, which are created to protect us from potential invasions of individual privacy, including either deliberately or accidentally by those collecting and processing personal data.

The initial building blocks behind today's privacy laws came in the form of privacy principles, such as those created by the United States with the Fair Information Practice Principles (FIPPs) in 1973.

Fair Information Practice Principles

It was in 1973 that the U.S. Department of Health, Education and Welfare codified the FIPPs[4], which provided best practices on the handling of personal data—referred to as personally identifiable information (PII)[5]. FIPPs were a first attempt to take something complex

---

3   United Nations (1948). Universal Declaration of Human Rights. http://www.un.org/en/udhrbook/pdf/udhr_booklet_en_web.pdf (last accessed 20 January 2018)
4   Homeland Security Privacy Office (1973). Fair Information Privacy Principles (FIPPs). https://www.dhs.gov/sites/default/files/publications/consolidated-powerpoint-final.pdf (last accessed 2 January 2017).
5   Any information that permits the identity of an individual to be directly or indirectly inferred, including any other information which is linked or linkable to that

and simplify it into actionable bullet-points. We provide this overview because privacy principles, laws and regulations devised globally thereafter were greatly influenced by FIPPs.

Within FIPPs, four principles on privacy are defined:

1. Rights of the Individual

2. Controls on the Information

3. Information Lifecycle

4. Management

Rights of the Individual

This principle states that organizations must provide notice about their privacy policies and how personal data is used. Choices should be presented to individuals on the collection, use, retention and sharing of personal data. It is here the concept of "opt in" and "opt out" consent was first presented to individuals.

Figure 1. FIPPs Rights of the Individual

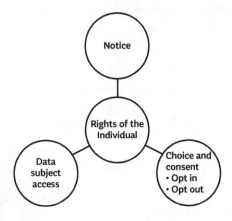

---

individual regardless of whether the individual is a U.S. citizen, lawful permanent resident, visitor to the U.S., or employee or contractor to the Department.

Controls on the Information

This refers to the protection of personal data with information security controls, and the responsibility of the organization to ensure that personal data is kept up to date, *i.e.* data quality is preserved.

Figure 2. FIPPs Controls on the Information

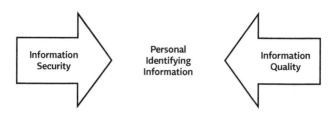

Information Lifecycle

This starts with data **collection**, and states that organizations that collect personal data should collect only what is needed for the purpose identified in the privacy notice. Organizations should only **use** personal data for the purposes described in the privacy notice; **retain** it for only as long as the purpose requires; and finally, **disclose** to third parties nothing outside of what is communicated within the privacy notice.

Figure 3. FIPPs Information Lifecycle

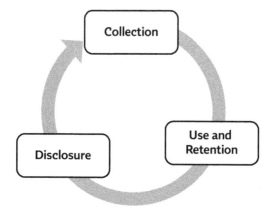

Management

The management principle covers what needs to be done to ensure the other three principles are implemented. This is to do with assigned **accountability** for the creation and application of privacy policies and procedures, along with **monitoring** and **enforcement** mechanisms to ensure that the organization is following what is written and communicated in privacy policies and procedures.

Figure 4. FIPPs Management

Accountability
Creation & application of privacy policies

Monitoring
Mechanism

Enforcement
Mechanism

The OECD Privacy Framework

In 1980, the Organization for Economic Co-operation and Development Guidelines Governing the Protection of Privacy and Transborder Flows of Personal Data (OECD Privacy Framework) guidelines were created, providing further foundations for privacy practices and regulations. These principles have become the basic building blocks of privacy laws in every country worldwide. For obvious cultural reasons, there are slight differences both in content and denomination, but from a theoretical perspective, they are the same. (Argentina and Mexico are just two countries with privacy laws containing principles very similar to those outlined in the OPEC Privacy Framework.) These principles could effectively be considered the lowest common denominator in privacy globally.

Collection Limitation Principle

There should be limits to the collection of personal data and any such data should be obtained by lawful and fair means and, where appropriate, with the knowledge or consent of the data subject.

Collect only what data is needed for the specified purpose, and if needed, get consent. For example, if your organization uses a web form to capture personal data in order to deliver a book ordered by a customer, the form should only include fields that are absolutely needed for the delivery of the book, nothing more. You could include a dropdown list of choices instead of a free-text box to restrict what the user is able to share. The collection must be strictly aligned to the specific purpose for collection, which is quite simply the delivery of the book.

Even at this stage, the need for openness and consent of the individual (i.e. data subject) is at the forefront. You will recognize distinct similarities with the first step (Collection) in the FIPPs Information Lifecycle privacy principle.

Data Quality Principle

> *Personal data should be relevant to the purposes for which they are to be used, and, to the extent necessary for those purposes, should be accurate, complete and kept up-to-date.*

If you are a security professional, you would be forgiven in mistaking this for integrity, as in the "Confidentiality, Integrity and Availability" (CIA) security triad which has provided the grounding rules on securing data for ages—even before the BS 7799 control framework became the adopted industry standard within information security (today known as ISO 27002, part of the ISO 27000 family).

What this principle is really about is in fact the quality of the data pertaining to the individual. This is personal data that changes during our lifetime. We move, we change names, we change our habits, and our health fluctuates. Our personal data must be kept up-to-date, and this is the responsibility of the organization or public entity that has collected the personal data. You can see that this principle is derived from the FIPPs "controls on the information" privacy principle, i.e., information quality.

Purpose Specification Principle

> *The purposes for which personal data are collected should be specified not later than at the time of data collection and the subsequent use limited to the fulfilment of those purposes or such others as not incompatible with those purposes, and as are specified on each occasion of change of purpose.*

There must be a specific purpose for the collection of personal data. If there is no purpose you should not be collecting it. It is that simple! Although, in practice, it is not.

Take the example that you buy a book on booksonline.com. The reason why you share your name and address is to deliver the book to your home. You may also share your credit card details, to pay for the book.

The purpose could purely be "client buys book," which combines both the "delivery of book" and "payment for book" into a single purpose. However, it would be more specific to create a separate purpose for each; the risks and collection channels over which personal data will travel over are distinctly different, and these implications become obvious when conducting a privacy impact assessment (PIA).

What is more, the purpose of personal data collection should be communicated to the data subject at the time of collection, whether through an external-facing privacy notice, or some other notice.

What is meant by "incompatible"? This means that any use must be compatible with the original stated purpose. See the next principle.

Use Limitation Principle

Personal data should be relevant to the purposes for which they are to be used, and, to the extent necessary for those purposes, should be accurate, complete and kept up-to-date.

How does your organization **use** personal data following its collection?

The purpose specifies **what** you are using personal data for, and the use is basically **how** you do this. For example, an individual orders a book on booksonline.com. The purpose "delivery of book" means that the department responsible for the delivery of the order receives only the personal data needed to get the book to the customer, e.g., name, address, book ordered, and delivery choices. For the related purpose "payment of book," there will also be a legal obligation to store financial data for 10-15 years, which is a legal requirement, and another use.

Personal data collected for the purpose of providing a harmonious user experience, such as the placing of cookies to store the customer's buying habits, is *not* compatible with either of the above purposes.

This data not needed to fulfil the delivery of the book, or to process the financial transaction. It will be used by marketing. In order to follow these rules, it is smart to create a separate purpose for marketing and the use of cookies. Each use must fall within the confines of each specified purpose.

If you take the FIPPs Information Lifecycle, it is easy to see how the Use Limitation Principle is a part of that lifecycle. Use is not only what you do with data, but what you do not do, including storing or sharing personal data, both internally and externally with third parties.

Security Safeguards Principle

Personal data should be protected by reasonable security safeguards against such risks as: loss or unauthorised access, destruction, use, modification or disclosure.

If you are an information security professional, you will have realized by now that privacy is much more than information security. Clearly, it is impossible to have privacy without information security; there must be adequate technical, management and organizational measures implemented to protect personal data. After all, information security is about the protection of personal data, and ensuring it is available when needed to minimize service disruptions

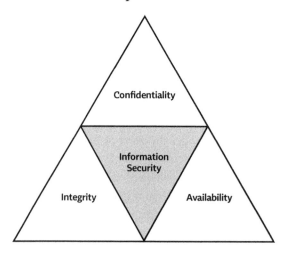

The challenge for information security professionals is that whenever new methods are developed for creating or collecting, storing, or transmitting information, these innovations are almost inevitably followed by methods of harnessing the new technologies and protecting the information they process. Since the 1990s, the confidentiality, integrity, and availability (CIA) model has been the *de facto* standard by which to design and build an organization's information security architecture.

The domain of information security has been around so long you would think, "it's not rocket science," but it is. "So much has changed in the way we store data, where we store it, how we transmit it, and how we secure it. Moreover, ensuring data security and protecting privacy is becoming harder as the information multiplies and is shared ever more widely around the world. The threats to information confidentiality, integrity, and availability have evolved into a vast collection of events, including accidental damage, destruction, theft, unintended or unauthorized modification, or other misuses from human or nonhuman threats," writes security engineer Georgie Pender-Bey.[6]

Openness Principle

There should be a general policy of openness about developments, practices and policies with respect to personal data. Means should be readily available of establishing the existence and nature of personal data, and the main purposes of their use, as well as the identity and usual residence of the data controller.

FIPPs considers openness under Right of Individual. An example of openness is the external-facing privacy notice that informs the data subject of the purpose for the collection of personal data, and what is done with it after use. There could be other legal obligations on reporting to national data protection authorities according to national privacy laws and regulations, such as with health care data, clinical trials, credit card data, etc.

---

6   Georgie Pender-Bey (2012). THE PARKERIAN HEXAD http://cs.lewisu.edu/
    mathcs/msisprojects/papers/georgiependerbey.pdf p5 (last accessed, 11 December
    2017)

An individual should have the right:

- *to obtain from a data controller, or otherwise, confirmation of whether or not the data controller has data relating to him;*

- *to have communicated to him, data relating to him, within a reasonable time, at a charge, if any, that is not excessive, in a reasonable manner, and in a form that is readily intelligible to him;*

- *to be given reasons if a request made under subparagraphs (a) and (b) is denied, and to be able to challenge such denial; and to challenge data relating to him and, if the challenge is successful to have the data erased, rectified, completed or amended.*

Individual Participation Principle

The expectation for public notice, data subject access, with choice and consent for the individual also stems from the FIPPs Right of Individual. The OECD principles extend these expectations so that the individual is able to request information about who is collecting their personal data, and what is being done with it. Moreover, the individual should have the right to request that personal data is amended/updated if the data quality principle is at issue, or erased if the use of personal data is not compatible with the purpose for collection.

A data controller should be accountable for complying with measures which give effect to the principles stated above.

Accountability Principle

Basically this means there needs to be evidence of data protection compliance and implementation of measures and policies to meet the requirements laid out in the principles, such as ensuring the rights of the data subject are responded to, etc.

Privacy Dilemmas

Every privacy law presents the challenge of balancing the right to a private life against national safety and commercial growth. Factors such as culture and political structure influence how privacy laws are implemented in those countries that have them.

What's more, every privacy law globally is challenged by realities of the so-called "Information Age"—a term coined at the beginning of this century that has grown to encompass the "Internet of Things" (IoT), "data analytics" and "Big Data." This has, over the last 30 years, unleashed a surveillance society: A multi-faceted beast that started its life in the form of cameras overlooking public spaces such as subways and football grounds (referred to as "Big Brother"), and has evolved to include a proliferation of personal data collection devices. Now we have the "Little Sister" phenomena: Sensors, GPS and location services running on mobile phones, smart watches, fitness trackers, and other wearables, and intelligent home systems have all extended the reach of surveillance to sousveillance and life-logging. As a consequence, personal data has become a tangible commodity which can be bought and sold if national privacy laws permit. It is the users of these devices that privacy laws are created to protect

What is Internet of Things (IoT)?

Wearables, intelligent homes, sensors, Global Positioning Systems (GPS), Location Based Services (LBS), the black box in your car, are all examples of the IoT. Personal data is being collected without the knowledge of the data subject. They are "passive" in the collection. Although the individual may have enabled collection through a wearable, an app on a mobile device, etc., they are not "active" in sharing their personal data. The individual is potentially unaware to the extent of personal data being collected in their environment which is becoming more and more ubiquitous.

Freedom of Speech versus Privacy

Some countries refer to this concept as freedom of speech, others use freedom of information or freedom of expression. For simplicity, we are using the term freedom of speech, but we refer to any such right.

One of the principal challenges of every country that has implemented privacy laws is how that law co-exists with freedom of speech protections. We need both in order for a democratic society to function effectively.

Safety and National Security versus Privacy

Society needs to be protected from illegal activities and potentially dangerous individuals and criminal organizations. This has been an ongoing discussion: How far can you go in the invasion of privacy in the name of law enforcement?

The GDPR has exemptions to the rights of the data subject (Individual Participation and Openness Principles) for law enforcement and national security activities. There are other laws controlling access by government authorities in their role as law enforcement and intelligence gathering agencies to personal data. In Article 6(e) of the GDPR you will find that "national interest" is a legal basis for processing.

Gross National Product (GNP) versus Privacy

It was mainly businesses, government authorities, law enforcement and national security agencies that lobbied for the flow of personal data. In order for society to function there needs to be controlled access by government authorities in their role as law enforcement and intelligence gathering.

On the other side have been privacy advocates, representatives on behalf of the data-subject and the data subjects themselves.

Table 1. Conflicting goals of data protection in the EU

Society needs to function		Right to privacy
Permit flow of personal data among member states	⟷	Protect the privacy of E.U. data subjects

How the GDPR deals with privacy dilemmas

The GDPR does its best to balance these conflicting dilemmas, starting by placing the individual at the center. Moreover, the legal text of the GDPR has shifted away from the analog world upon which its predecessor directive was based (Data Protection Directive, 1995) and toward the digitized world of today. It also provides a foundation for the future. This makes the GDPR a complex piece of legislation and despite the voice of some critics, it is nonetheless a piece of legal art of which we can, within the EU, be proud. As with any piece of art, it has its purpose. It is written by lawyers for lawyers. As with any law, it will be tested up to the highest courts within the EU during its lifetime. It is a law that sets the rules of play pertaining to data protection within the EU. What we have is a baby with a strong DNA, and we will see case law determine its character during its lifetime.

Channels of privacy invasion

These "privacy types," representing different channels for invasion or breach, were originally identified by Privacy International more than 10 years ago. While no reference can be found on their website today, the categorizations live on in privacy impact assessment guides offered by places such as Ontario, Canada, and Victoria, Australia (along with an additional type referred to as location privacy).

Privacy Type	Source
Information Privacy	Privacy International
Bodily Privacy	Privacy International
Territorial Privacy	Privacy International
Communications Privacy	Privacy International
Location Privacy	Victoria, Australia PIA

The document created by the Privacy Impact Assessment Framework (PIAF)[7] consortium and prepared for the European Commission

---

7   Homeland Security Privacy Office (1973). Fair Information Privacy Principles (FIPPs). https://www.dhs.gov/sites/default/files/publications/consolidated-powerpoint-final.pdf (last accessed 2 January 2017). Privacy Impact Assessment

Directorate-General for Justice in 2011, which compared privacy impact assessment guidelines internationally, recommends the use of these five privacy types, which consider privacy beyond information privacy.

We will now discuss the privacy types in more detail.

Information privacy

Information privacy protects personal information and involves the establishment of rules governing the collection and handling of personal data such as credit information and medical and government records.

Information privacy is the most well understood part of privacy because it was around even before digitization took over our lives; it includes personal data that you share with your employer, health care provider, local government authorities, banks, insurance agents, etc. It is the sensitive data that has been collected on us, traditionally in paper format and migrated into a digital format over the last 20-30 years.

Information privacy in practice is when you fill in a form with personal data. It could be to order a book, or to register for a newsletter. You, as the data subject, are *active* in sharing your personal data, and typically aware of what you are sharing.

Bodily privacy

Bodily privacy protects the integrity of the physical person against invasive procedures such as genetic tests, drug testing and cavity searches.

From biometrics to DNA or drug tests to body scans, technology that just 10 years ago was the content of sci-fi films (or limited to the realms of law enforcement) has now infiltrated our daily lives. We use our fingerprint to use our iPhone, send our DNA to be analysed for hereditary diseases, submit to random testing for substance abuse in the workplace, and enter body scanners when we travel at airports.

Biometrics

It has become the standard to include biometrics in our passports and ID cards. Biometrics were once considered very intrusive to our privacy, although the use of biometrics is becoming more commonplace nowadays.

Framework (2011). A Privacy Impact Assessment Framework for data protection and privacy rights. http://www.vub.ac.be/LSTS/pub/Dehert/507.pdf (last accessed 27th November 2016)

A biometric is a physical and unique characteristic of an individual. Examples include your fingerprints, hands, face, irises, gait and behavior. The use of a fingerprint to access your iPhone is an example of biometric authentication as is the use of biometrics (both fingerprint and iris) as a gun safety feature, ensuring the firearm can only be used by the authorised owner and/or user.

Some countries are using facial recognition systems, which match the biometrics on your passport with what is returned by scanning devices, at their borders. If the match is positive you are permitted through.

DNA

Did you know that your DNA is sensitive data? And that each person's DNA is unique except for identical twins?

Not only does genetic information provide something like a fingerprint through variations in genetic sequences, it also provides a growing amount of information on genetic diseases and predispositions. Errors in the genetic code are responsible for an estimated 3,000-4,000 hereditary diseases.

Territorial privacy

Territorial privacy protects personal space, objects and behavior; consider the setting of limits on intrusion in the domestic sphere and other environments such as the workplace or other public and private spaces. Such intrusions can include searches, video surveillance and ID checks.

Surveillance

George Orwell's book *1984* predicted a Big Brother state as the fate for our society. In reality, our society has evolved into more of a Little Brother/Sister state. Surveillance has become widespread, but is not government dominated; rather, it is disparate and disconnected. Video surveillance through CCTV (closed-circuit TV) is used to monitor public and private spaces worldwide. There are laws in most countries restricting the use of CCTV. The requester must have a solid reason for installing CCTV cameras, and must get approval from the relevant government authorities.

"Sousveillance"

Up until 10 years ago, surveillance was conducted only in the name of public safety and law enforcement, but that was until the smartphone hit the streets and brought us into a new dimension of "sousveillance."

The term sousveillance is derived from the contrasting French words *sur*, meaning "above", and *sous*, meaning "below." While "surveillance" suggests an "eye in the sky" watching from above, "sousveillance" denotes bringing the camera down to human level (an individual is watching, rather than government authorities or private industry). The first person to start the trend of sousveillance was Canadian researcher and inventor Steve Mann, who has been dubbed "The Father of Wearable Computing." He's been walking around with a camera strapped to his head recording his life since the 1980s. Since that time, wearables have evolved from large and clumsy to the elegant Google Glass that can be purchased today. Furthermore, sousveillance is even what we are doing with our mobile phones, taking photos and video often without the knowledge of the data subject.

ID Checks

An ID card is required in order to conduct an ID check. Your ID card is a legal document providing evidence that you are who you say you are. Some ID cards created by government authorities include biometric data.

ID checks are done to validate your identity by border controls at the airport and to check you are of a legal age upon the purchase of restricted items such as tobacco and alcohol, for example.

Communications privacy

Communications privacy protects against eavesdropping on mail, telephone calls, email and other forms of communication.

Any voice communication that runs over telephone networks is included; this not only includes contents of voice conversations but also something called metadata.

Every time you make a call, information about that call—including who you call and how long you are connected—is stored for a short time by the telecommunications provider as metadata. There are laws implemented in most countries globally requiring operators to store metadata for an extended period of time in the name of law enforcement. Many of the international laws on wiretapping date back to a series of seminars hosted by the FBI in 1993 at its research facility in Quantico, Virginia. The seminar was called the *International Law Enforcement Telecommunications Seminar (ILETS)* together with representatives from Canada, Hong Kong, Australia and the EU. The result was an international standard called the *International Requirements for Interception*, which was adopted by the European Union in 1995. This standard sets out a legal requirement for all telecommunication providers and equipment manufacturers to build surveillance capabilities into all telephone systems.

Location privacy

Location privacy protects against surveillance via anything "smart" that you wear or use. Such technology is a ubiquitous part of our modern lives: location based services (LBS), Global Positioning Systems (GPS) and Radio Frequency Identifiers (RFID) used by wearables and sensors in your home, workplace and basically everywhere you move around.

In this case, the user is passive in the collection of personal data. This means that once the service is enabled, the user of the service does not need to do anything to facilitate data collection. This is one of the characteristics of the Internet of Things (IoT).

Global Positioning System (GPS)

GPS is something we have been using traditionally in our cars to find the right way to our destinations. However, its uses are expanding—tracking taxis or delivery vehicles, for example. This data is stored in a black box, which can be used following an accident. The speed of a car at impact together with GPS data is revealing.

Location Based Services (LBS)

With the download of an app on your mobile device, tracking can pinpoint your location at any given moment in time. You can use such services to find a coffee shop in the local vicinity, or the closest airport lounge.

Radio Frequency Identifiers (RFID)

RFID is a technology that is turning virtually every item in our static ecosystem—from your coffee machine to your clothes to the lighting in your house—into a living ecosystem, converting personal habits and activities into a digital format, hence one that can be intelligently analyzed, correlated and mined. RFID tags today are embedded in items, clothes, living animals and individuals. The sensors have uses ranging from helping your car with parking to assisting in search and rescue missions (with the embedding of an RFID chip in ski and mountain wear).

The combined use of GPS and sensors is also leading a revolution in driverless cars, enabling them to be tracked in real time from an offsite control center as well as helping to monitor conditions and control speed, all without any driver input.

What about cookies?

One of the most pervasive privacy invasions not covered here is the use of "cookies." Cookies are downloaded onto your computer to keep a track of what you are doing when you browse a website. If we were to define the type of privacy that involves cookies, it could be called "device privacy."

Cookies collect personal data of which you are not aware, you just see the results, e.g. books you have browsed when visiting an online bookstore. They were developed to enhance the user experience, but today their use is abused. Cookies and more will be covered in the GDPR's ePrivacy Regulation due to replace the ePrivacy Directive. The timeline for that, as of this writing, is unknown. The text has not yet been finalized, but what is certain is that "choice" will be key. To protect device privacy, a user of a web service should not be forced to accept cookies outside of what is absolutely necessary to provide that service.

Digital Personal Data Properties

Digitized data has properties[8] beyond those that were considered before society went digital and online. Irrespective of whether personal data is user-generated or not, four properties[9] apply:

- Digital persistence,
- Replicability,
- Searchability
- Invisible audiences

In the application to personal data we have adapted the concept and appended a fifth property: unintended processing.

Digital persistence

Everything you share online is digitally stored on multiple servers somewhere. Why multiple servers? All data digitally stored is normally "mirrored" in order to meet availability requirements, e.g., if one server becomes unavailable or overloaded with traffic, a mirror site will take over the request from the user. Additionally, all data is stored on backup media somewhere. This data will persist until the media is overwritten, and this should be determined by a security policy on media rotation.

The persistence property is a trigger for the Right to Erasure within the new GDPR. Execution of this right needs to be reasonable. The question of personal data stored on backup tapes is common; this can be dealt with by following the industry standards for information security pertaining to backup and media rotation. For example, every three months, backup tapes are re-used, i.e., overwritten.

Searchability

This takes us to the Right to Be Forgotten (RTBF), as defined in the GDPR. When you are searching for data pertaining to an individual online, the search engine, using its complex analytics and small virtual

---

8   Danah boyd, a well-known researcher and expert on young people and how they use social media, defined that the "mediated public" was referring to user-generated content created in online spaces.

9   Boyd, D. (1998) https://www.danah.org/papers/TakenOutOfContext.html (accessed 7th May 2017).

spiders, finds all related data. You can liken this to the index in a book. The Right to Be Forgotten does not remove contents of the book in this example—that's the Right to Erasure. RTBF removes the specific index which references a specific individual in the book. The Right to Erasure has been around since the EU's Data Protection Directive of 1995, stating that personal data must be erased if a specific purpose for processing is lacking.

The most publicized driver behind the RTBF can be found in the judgment of Google Spain SL and Google Inc. v Agencia Española de Protección de Datos (AEPD) and Mario Costeja González (C-131/12). The press was for a time full of articles and opinions about whether RTBF is a practice that inhibits the freedom of expression, or whether individuals should be free to exercise this right.

The European Court of Justice judgement pertains purely to search results and auto-complete functionality within the Google search engine. It is not about the original content. What this ruling is about is search engine results and intelligent auto-complete on searches for personal data, linked to an individual who is an EU data subject, that has passed its "sell by date." What this means in practice is that if something is published in the press, it remains printed and searchable. This ruling is not about re-writing history (as in George Orwell's horror scenario, "1984"). Everything remains published in the press. If you want to find it you just need to know exactly where to look. In our book example, this would be the page number referenced by the deleted index.

Replicability

Digital content can be copied; this means that you can copy personal data from one place and paste it into another place, such as Customer Relationship Management (CRM) sales data copied into the CRM app on a mobile device, or data copied from an approved business system to a USB stick. Copied data is difficult to control, in that it is difficult to determine whether the content has been changed—presenting risks to quality of data.

In the context of personal data collected within your organization, personal data collected for a specific purpose must be used purely for this specific purpose. Personal data collected to deliver a book to a customer cannot be copied and used for marketing.

Invisible data, or the "unknown unknowns"

It is the CxO's worst nightmare: Where is personal data being collected and processed within the organization? Which employees have copied (replicability) personal data onto mobile devices or USB sticks without even being aware themselves that it is personal data? If you ask for a definition of personal data, many individuals will respond with PII (personal identifiable information) or some simple examples, such as name, address, IP address, or health data. Very few would have any idea that the definition of personal data is any data which can be linked directly or indirectly to a living individual. It is not uncommon that invisible personal data has attained a state of digital immortality (digital persistence) thanks to human nature being what it is and individuals taking a "keep just-in-case" approach over safe erasure.

Unintended processing

The mere act of storing personal data is an act of processing personal data. Everything your organization does with personal data, even the process of backing up data, is processing. Archiving personal data is processing. All personal data is processed in some form or other until it is securely erased from every system.

Privacy is individual-centric!

If you have not worked it out by now, privacy is "individual-centric"! Let's start with ownership of personal data. Does this really matter? Yes, because by exploring this question you can weed out the real privacy experts from those who claim they are experts.

Who owns personal data?

The answer to this question is fundamental to privacy and data protection principles, not just the GDPR. If you get this wrong, you will get it all wrong. The funny thing is that most IT and information security experts will get it wrong. This is not surprising because they spend most of their working life protecting the intellectual property of their employers and clients, so it would never occur to them that personal data stored by the company (data controller) does not in fact belong to the organization, but to the data subjects themselves.

The data subject in effect loans their personal data to whichever legal entity is required in order to fulfil a specific purpose. You could liken this to lending your car to a friend. You would expect at least the following:

- That your friend would take care of the car, not to scratch or dent it.

- If anything goes wrong that they inform you immediately.

- Your friend would use it only for the purpose they stated at the outset, and if it was used for something more, that they would be transparent that this was the case.

- Your friend would pay for fuel used.

- The car would be returned once the purpose for lending it was fulfilled.

To take another example. If you were to buy a book at your favorite online bookstore, you will share your address with the store so that they can deliver your book. Once the book has been delivered and the purpose fulfilled, the online bookstore should delete your personal data unless you have agreed that they can keep it in their records, i.e. to save you from having to type it in again when you buy another book.

Learning Activity

For discussion in groups.

#	Privacy Foundations
1	Iris scanners (biometrics) are used by your organization to permit access to restricted areas that contain radioactive materials. Is biometrics personal data? Provide justification for your response.
2	The head of security wants to place surveillance cameras in the office space, including the corridors leading to the restrooms. As the Chief Operating Officer, how will you deal with this request?
3	The FindMyFriends App is available on both iPhone and Android. What are the most probable collection channels used to provide the service to its users? Is the user *active* or *passive* in the collection of personal data?
4	ACME AB has a jobs@acme.se address configured to receive applications for a jobs that have been posted on its website. HR has configured this as a group mailbox that syncs the emails received to their local mailbox stored on their PC. As a privacy specialist, do you see a problem with this practice?
5	Learning Books AB is collecting customers' names and addresses when they order books online. The marketing department is using this data for a new marketing campaign. As a privacy professional, how would you explain to marketing and management that this is not allowed?

CHAPTER 2

The GDPR

What it means after May 25, 2018

The GDPR is the first privacy law in the EU to be graced with a strong set of teeth. In all its glory, it will be without a doubt the strongest privacy law globally. It empowers supervisory authorities to impose fines for non-compliance, and in the event of a personal data breach, to collect up to 4 percent of annual turnover or 20 million euros, whichever is higher. Even the public sector is not exempt (although the fines imposed here are not aligned to turnover, as theoretically they have none as public-sector organizations).

The GDPR must be applied after May 25, 2018, when existing data protection laws in each EU member state will become obsolete. Implementation is not the end of the story, because further molding will occur in time, according to case law—when, for example, a data subject (or group of individuals) sues a private or public enterprise pertaining to the misuse of their personal data.

Compromises (or "derogations")

During the negotiations, in order to reach a final text, member states were afforded some flexibility to add or modify certain provisions of the GDPR to fit local needs and laws.[1] The result is around 50-60 possibilities for member states to adopt these "national derogations."

---

1   GDPR, Recital 10.

Only a few will be examined here.

Lawfulness of processing

All member states are given the right to further specify the lawfulness of processing from the more general conditions the regulation establishes. Some areas where this might be necessary are specified in the regulation,[2] i.e., to establish:

- Specifications for determining the controller.
- The entities to which the personal data may be disclosed.
- The purpose limitations.
- The storage period.
- Other measures to ensure lawful and fair processing.

Special categories of personal data (sensitive personal data)

Let us start by asking you a question: What is sensitive information? Yes, it is defined in the regulation, but in reality, the answer—more than anything else in the regulation—might be different based on the culture and background of the person responding. This context is very different in Sweden, Romania and Portugal, for example. In some countries, such as Sweden, most people are willing to share information and are used to authorities being open to sharing information with whomever asks. This is logical in Sweden, given its history of very strong workers' unions and strong employment laws. The UK public, meanwhile, has actively fought against the implementation of a national ID system, seeing it as a control mechanism of government authorities.[3] The Brits just aren't as trusting of government authorities. Levels of reluctance and skepticism about sharing information span a wide range. We can also see a clear difference emerging between generations. It remains to see how coming generations think of their personal data.

In light of the above, it can be anticipated that some member states will exercise their right to adopt national derogations around sensitive

2   GDPR, Recital 10.
3   Karen Lawrence Öqvist (2009). Virtual Shadows: Your Privacy in the Information Society. British Computer Society. P47

data. In recital 52, the GDPR outlines circumstances when member states may derogate from the prohibition on processing special categories of data, including:

- In the field of employment law.

- Social protection law including pensions.

- For health security (monitoring and alert purposes).

- For prevention or control of communicable diseases and other serious threats to health.

Human resources and employee data

First some basic facts. Most companies have employees. In a group of companies, it is not uncommon to have employees across a number of legal entities. Normally the legal entity where a specific data subject is employed is considered data controller. In a pan-European or global enterprise this means there will be a number of controllers regulated by different jurisdictions. Keeping track of differences is thus of great importance. According to article 88 "[m]ember States may, by law or by collective agreements, provide for more specific rules to ensure the protection of the rights and freedoms in respect of the processing of employees' personal data in the employment context..." It is worth noting that the text mentions not only member state law, but also collective agreements, including "works agreements."[4] Some of the circumstances when member states' specific regulations may apply is in processing for the following purposes:

- Recruitment.

- Performance of the contract of employment.

- Management, planning and organization of work.

- Equality and diversity in the workplace.

- Health and safety at work.

- Protection of employer's or customer's property.

- Exercise and enjoyment of employees.

---

4   Recital 155.

- Rights and benefits related to employment.

- The termination of the employment relationship.

In addition, member states may also provide for specific rules on the processing of employees' personal data in the employment context on the basis of the consent of the employees.[5] But it is our recommendation not to rely on consent in the employment relationship.

Parental consent

Specific requirements apply to information society services and data processing when children are involved. If the child is below the age of 16 years, such processing shall be lawful only if and to the extent that consent is given or authorized by the holder of parental responsibility over the child.[6] But member states may adopt national specific laws with a lower age for a child to give valid consent for processing. The lowest age a member state may adopt for this purpose is 13 years old. It is anticipated that some member states will use this opportunity to adopt lower thresholds accordingly, empowering children to give consent from the age of 13, 14 or 15. For instance, 13 is currently the recommended age by the UK Information Commissioner's Office. In Sweden, the Swedish Data Protection Authority also has a 13-year-old threshold, but also explicitly states that it depends on both the data processed and the purpose. In November 2016, the Irish government launched a consultation to seek the views on the statutory age of consent threshold under this article.[7] Similar initiatives can be expected in other member states.

As information society services often direct their services towards a broad public, both domestic and international, these companies are up for a challenge, both in terms of what age threshold should be applied and how to assess the age of the user.

---

5 GDPR, Recital 155.
6 GDPR, Article 8.
7 http://www.justice.ie/en/JELR/Consultation_paper_Digital_Age_of_Consent.
    pdf/Files/Consultation_paper_Digital_Age_of_Consent.pdf

Privacy vs Data Protection

The GDPR uses the term "data protection" *not* "privacy" or "data privacy," which are used outside of the European Union (EU).

Privacy concepts that have been adopted as industry best practices globally, such as Privacy Impact Assessments (PIA) and Privacy by Design (PbD) have been rebranded as Data Protection Impact Assessment (DPIA) and Data Protection by Design (DPbD) in the GDPR.

This presents some challenges:

- IT and security experts who have worked on data protection projects, e.g., data loss prevention (DLP), data classification, etc., think that these are GDPR compliance. They may believe that GDPR compliance is a subset of security compliance. This has resulted in misunderstandings, and "the blind" false GDPR experts leading "the blind" clients into their security-colored glasses of GDPR compliance.

- Rolling out a global privacy program to national jurisdictions outside of the EU causes confusion in that "privacy" is used generically globally, but "data protection" is used within the EU. The highest bar in privacy compliance globally is within the EU (which means that global entities must meet this bar); however, to force GDPR language on the rest of the world would create confusion and friction between organizations within the EU and outside of the EU.

- GDPR does not resonate with employees. They do not understand what GDPR is, but "privacy" they can wrap their heads around. Whether the employee is an EU citizen or not is irrelevant. When it comes to rolling out privacy awareness outside of the EU within a global organization, it does not make sense to refer to this training as "GDPR awareness training." In fact, requests received so far from global organizations have specified that they want no mention of GDPR in what they call "privacy awareness training."

For these reasons, this book uses the terms "privacy" or "data privacy" over "data protection" throughout except when it discusses specifics to the GDPR.

GDPR made simple

Material & Territorial Scope

To whom and what does the EU GDPR apply? This is where we look at the scope of the GDPR. Just as you need to scope any project or activity, the law also has a scope of applicability. There are two parameters: material scope and territorial scope. Simply put, "material" is the "what?" And "territorial" is the "where?"

Material Scope

What it says about material scope is that it "applies to the processing of personal data wholly or partly by automated means and to the processing other than by automated means of personal data which form part of a filing system or are intended to form part of a filing system."

What this means is that it applies to all personal data whether it is stored and processed using digital techniques or not. It includes personal data:

- Stored electronically somewhere.

- Printed on paper and stored in a filing cabinet.

Without being dragged too much into the 'legal speak' we should mention the two most significant exceptions:

- "Processing of personal data for purely personal or household activity." What this means is that "the rules don't apply to data processed by an individual for purely personal reasons or for activities carried out in one's home, provided there is no connection to a professional or commercial activity. When an individual uses personal data outside the personal sphere," then the GDPR applies.[8]

- Processing "by authorities for the purposes of the prevention, investigation, detection or prosecution of criminal offenses," i.e processing by the police or intelligence agencies.[9] This processing is instead regulated in an EU directive[310].

---

8 European Commission. What does the General Data Protection Regulation (GDPR) govern? https://ec.europa.eu/info/law/law-topic/data-protection/reform/what-does-general-data-protection-regulation-gdpr-govern_en (last accessed 24 February 2018)

9 Article 2 2.

10 Directive (EU) 2016/680 of the European Parliament and of the Council of 27

Territorial Scope

How far does the GDPR stretch geographically? It applies to every organization processing personal data of data subjects residing in the Union, even if the organization is operating from an establishment outside of the EU. This is irrespective of whether the offered service is free or not, and it includes the monitoring of behavior[11].

When the regulation applies:

- Your company offers a cloud service providing HR services, which is operating with an establishment based outside the EU. It targets mainly or partially English-speaking business in the EU.

When the regulation does not apply:

- Your company offers a cloud service providing HR services with an establishment based outside the EU. Its clients can use its services when they travel to other countries, including within the EU. Provided your company doesn't specifically target its services at individuals in the EU, it is not subject to the rules of the GDPR.

- Your company is based in Argentina and offers goods to consumers in Argentina and Mexico. Your web page is in Spanish only, and you *only* offer shipping to Argentina and Mexico. Even though theoretically a Spanish resident could order goods from you and redirect the parcel via a postal address in Argentina or Mexico this was never your purpose and therefore GDPR is not applicable.

Key GDPR definitions

Just to get you started, here are some simple explanations of essential GDPR terminology:

- **Personal data** is any data which can directly or indirectly link to a specific individual (from the moment of birth until death).

April 2016 on the protection of natural persons with regard to the processing of personal data by competent authorities for the purposes of the prevention, investigation, detection or prosecution of criminal offences or the execution of criminal penalties, and on the free movement of such data, and repealing Council Framework Decision 2008/977/JHA.

11 This is in legal terms called "extraterritorial jurisdiction."

- **Processing** is anything done with data from the time of collection. Processing only stops when personal data is securely destructed or truly anonymized.

- **Controller** is the legal entity that decides the purpose for the collection and processing of personal data.

- **Processor** is the legal entity which processes personal data on behalf of the controller. A processor should do only what it is tasked to do by the controller, nothing more, at the risk of becoming a controller with the same liabilities.[12]

The full legal definitions, if not provided in the body of this book, are provided in Appendix A. You will be relieved to find that in fact the legal text, at a first glance, is not weighed down by too much legal jargon. The authors have done an awesome job in making it easy to understand. There are some phrases that are stumbling blocks, e.g., "incompatible with those purposes," but even this you could, as a non-legal expert, decipher its meaning. A word of warning: Beware, there is significant meaning behind the text that only the legal professional can see.

Articles and Recitals, what are they?

There are a few iPhone and Android apps appearing on the market that you can use to refer to the GDPR. Some even have matched Recitals to Articles, which is a relief, because the Articles state what is law and the Recitals provide some explanations on the thinking behind the Articles. In the full document, the Recitals are confusingly listed in no apparent order (for a non-legal professional).

GDPR tools in your pocket

One particularly good app is that provided by Fieldfisher, as it lists the Recitals together with the Articles.

---

12 *See* SWIFT case 2009 (https://www.lexology.com/library/detail. aspx?g=853bdcbb-32e6-4e72-88c0-89376ec6c60b)

What is personal data?

The GDPR definition of personal data

> GDPR definition: "personal data" means any information relating to an identified or identifiable natural person ("data subject"); an identifiable natural person is one who can be identified, directly or indirectly, in particular by reference to an identifier such as a name, an identification number, location data, an online identifier or to one or more factors specific to the physical, physiological, genetic, mental, economic, cultural or social identity of that natural person.

In short, personal data is any data which can be linked directly and/or indirectly to a natural person. A natural person is a living individual; from when an individual is born and until death.

Be aware that just because an individual is not protected before birth or after death, does not mean there is no protection. You may need to check other laws.

Sensitive personal data

Sensitive personal data is any personal data revealing racial or ethnic origin, political opinions, religious or philosophical beliefs, trade union membership, genetic data, biometric data processed for the purpose of uniquely identifying a natural person, data concerning health, or data concerning a natural person's sex life or sexual orientation. In the GDPR it is called "special categories of data."

Identifiability

Personal data can have strong or weak identifiability. An example of a strong identifier is your passport and your identification number, and even your name. Examples of weak identifiers are personal data points that need to be combined with another identifier in order for the natural person to be identifiable. There is also something called quasi-identifiers which is "data that can be combined with external knowledge to link data to an individual."[13]

---

13 Chris Clifton (2014). Introduction to IT Privacy: A Handbook for Technologists, Identity and Anonymity. IAPP Publication P149.

Anonymized data

Personal data stops being considered personal data in the GDPR once it is securely anonymized. Anonymized data is personal data that cannot be linked or traced back to a natural person. If it is possible to reverse anonymized data back to the data subject, it is not anonymized, it is pseudonymized. Pseudonymized data is still considered personal data, and the same rules apply to pseudonymized data as to personal data.

The difference between anonymization and pseudonymization is that the latter is reversible, the former is not.

About the GDPR principles

The GDPR is actually not that difficult to read, although to understand it is something else. A single word could mean something completely different to a legal professional than to a non-legal professional. The problem is that however beautiful the legal text is, it is not possible to use it as an implementation tool on an operational level.

Some typical real-life examples are:

- In order to implement data protection by design and as a default across your organization, it means that the GDPR language needs to be understood by all, from those doing testing, up to board level. Yet the language in Article 5(1)(a) is not specific or tangible for those who don't have a legal education in data protection. They will not see what is written behind the two simple words "lawfully" and "fairly." They will take it as per se, and as such, misunderstandings will occur between legal and the rest of the business.

- Due to the lack of a common understanding, the business will not listen to the experts, who are the legal team.

- If the business does listen to legal, they may implement GDPR in a way that is incorrect, e.g., conduct privacy impact assessment by IT system, create a "breach notification policy" instead of a "personal data breach notification policy," or implement privacy as a subset of cybersecurity compliance, all because they misunderstood the message from legal.

The GDPR principles relating to the processing of personal data (Article 5) have created any number of common implementation challenges, as outlined below.

Personal data shall be:

(a) *processed lawfully, fairly and in a transparent manner in relation to the data subject ('lawfulness, fairness and transparency');*

Take just the first two requirements in Article 5 (1) (a): "processed lawfully, fairly." In order to be lawful and fair in the processing of personal data, you need to read and interpret, in a legal way, the whole GDPR. This is a difficult one for compliance/IT guys who will be scratching their heads over how to implement this provision. That is why (in this book) the OECD Privacy Principles comprise the recommended implementation framework for privacy compliance.

(b) *collected for specified, explicit and legitimate purposes and not further processed in a manner that is incompatible with those purposes; further processing for archiving purposes in the public interest, scientific or historical research purposes or statistical purposes shall, in accordance with Article 89(1), not be considered to be incompatible with the initial purposes ('purpose limitation');*

The main challenge here is that it discusses processing in the same sentence as collection and purpose. This causes confusion in project scoping, as processing is anything done with personal data, including storage on archive media. If you have not scoped your project carefully around the specific purpose; defined roles (controller, processor); and identified accountable parties first, you could end up creating personal data-flows through to back-up media when your IT environment is in fact outsourced. If your IT environment is outsourced, data privacy risks probably need to focus on processing agreements and GDPR legal clauses, e.g., compliance with ISO 27001.

It is* not *legal to share personal data,* even internally, *unless it is absolutely necessary!

(c) *adequate, relevant and limited to what is necessary in relation to the purposes for which they are processed ('data minimisation');*

This is a fairly straightforward concept. Do not share personal data, even internally, unless it is absolutely necessary. The use of personal data must correlate directly with the purpose for collection, or there must be a legal basis for processing (Article 6, which will be covered later).

(d) *accurate and, where necessary, kept up to date; every reasonable step must be taken to ensure that personal data that are inaccurate, having regard to the purposes for which they are processed, are erased or rectified without delay ('accuracy');*

This is where the protection of personal data extends into data transparency. All data subjects have the right to challenge the accuracy of their data and request controller updates, if it is not accurate. This is one of the reasons why you must implement a personal data inventory so you have a mapping of personal data metadata to the actual data embedded in business processes. Or you could give the data subject a self-service portal so they are in control of their data; at least on the outward-facing component. In any case, a new role is surfacing called DSAR (Data Subject Access Request) Specialist, providing a human interface for this function.

(e) *kept in a form which permits identification of data subjects for no longer than is necessary for the purposes for which the personal data are processed; personal data may be stored for longer periods insofar as the personal data will be processed solely for archiving purposes in the public interest, scientific or historical research purposes*

*or statistical purposes in accordance with Article 89(1)
subject to implementation of the appropriate technical
and organizational measures required by this Regulation
in order to safeguard the rights and freedoms of the data
subject ('storage limitation');*

If you store personal data beyond the purpose for
collection, it needs to be anonymized. Anonymized
data is no longer personal data according to the GDPR.
Pseudonymized data is still considered personal data
as it is reversible! There are some exceptions on the
use of pseudonymized data, e.g., clinical trials in
pharmaceuticals.

Anonymised data is not personal data. *Pseudonymised data
is personal data because it can be reversed back again.*

(f) *processed in a manner that ensures appropriate security
of the personal data, including protection against
unauthorised or unlawful processing and against
accidental loss, destruction or damage, using appropriate
technical or organizational measures ('integrity and
confidentiality').*

This is pretty straightforward for the information
security and compliance experts among us. By
following industry standards, any business can comply
with this requirement; although "absolute security" is
impossible, one can demonstrate "due diligence." This
requirement is one of the most important for those
acting as a processor. Much of this is further elaborated
in Article 32.

(g) *The controller shall be responsible for, and be able
to demonstrate compliance with, paragraph 1
('accountability').*

Evidence is the key word here and you will need to be
able to demonstrate compliance to the supervisory
authority upon request after May 25, 2018.

This is only possible if you have rolled out a privacy program that assigns accountability at all levels—every employee has a role to play. Apart from following industry standards, e.g., ITIL/ITSM, ISO 27001, etc., you may need to assign a Data Protection Officer, and have the policies translated into actionable procedures at the operational level across your organization, demonstrating data protection by design as the default mode of operation across your organization.

What you should have as a takeaway from this section, is to know when to call in the legal troops, because they do intuitively offer a legal interpretation of what they read.

The rights of the data subject

What is different in the GDPR as compared to other privacy laws globally is that it has actually given rights to the data subject on anything concerning their personal data. There are whole sections dedicated to this; the concept is moreover woven into most of the legal text within the GDPR. Consequently, the data subject has a lot of rights that are legally enforceable. The rights of the data subject correlate directly with the "individual participation" OECD principle.

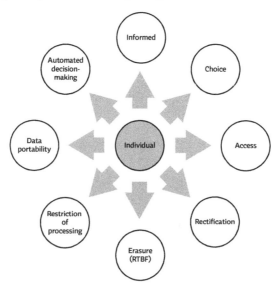

The data subject has the:

- *Right to be Informed* on what their personal data is being used for. These rights differ depending on whether personal data is collected directly or indirectly.

- *Right of Access* to personal data that they've shared; if you take the book example, a "self-service" portal would serve this function fine.

- *Right to Rectification* so that if a legal entity has your personal data it must be kept up-to-date.

- *Right to Erasure* if the purpose has been fulfilled (let's say you don't want to buy any more books from the online book store we used in the previous example).

- *Right to the Restriction of Processing* is more complex; if for example there is a court case in progress, even if the purpose for collection has been fulfilled, your personal data will be effectively frozen for a period of time.

- *Right to Data Portability* means all personal data must be kept in a machine-readable format that you should be able to download, and those storing your data must respect your request that it be moved to another provider, e.g., let's say you want to move your bank account from Bank A to Bank B.

- *Right to Object* to what is being done with your personal data.

- *Rights relating to automated individual decision-making, including profiling*, which is linked to big data analytics—you have the right to object to decisions made that are wholly automated.

Right to be Informed

The data subject has the Right to be Informed at the time that personal data was obtained from the data subject, hence the information should be provided at the time of collection. This right hooks into the "openness" OECD principle.

The GDPR differentiates the Right to be Informed based on whether the personal data was obtained directly[14] or indirectly[15] from the data subject as shown in Table 2: The Right to be Informed.

If the personal data was not obtained directly from the data subject, the information should be provided:

- Within a reasonable period after obtaining the personal data (at the latest within one month), and having regard to the specific circumstances in which the personal data are processed.

- If the personal data are to be used for communication with the data subject, at the latest at the time of the first communication to that data subject.

- If a disclosure to another recipient is envisaged, at the latest when the personal data are first disclosed.

---

14 GDPR Article 13
15 GDPR Article 14

Table 2. The Right to be Informed

Information to be given	Collected directly from data subject	Collected indirectly from data subject
The identity and the contract details of the controller and, where applicable, of the controller's representative	Y	Y
The contact details details of the data protection officer, where applicable;	Y	Y
The purposes of the processing as well as the legal basis for the processing	Y	Y
Legitimate interests pursued by the controller or by a third party (where applicable)	Y	Y
The recipients or categories of recipients of the personal data, if any;	Y	Y
Where applicable, the fact that the controller intends to transfer personal data to a third country or international organization (including reference to mechanism used for transfers)	Y	Y
Retention period	Y	Y
Notice on the data subject's rights	Y	Y
Right to withdraw consent, where applicable	Y	Y
The right to lodge a complaint with a supervisory authority	Y	Y
Whether the provision of personal data is part of a statutory or contractual requirement/obligation and possible consequences of failing to provide the data	Y	
The existence of automated decion-making, including profiling, and information on how those decisions are made	Y	Y
Categories of data	Y	Y

Right of Access

The data subject has the right to access[16] their personal data.

Following an access request to the controller, the controller has an obligation to:

- Respond to a data subject within one month from the receipt of the request.

- Provide the personal data they process.

- Provide free of charge.[17]

- Provide in a commonly used electronic form, unless otherwise requested.

Finally, the Right of Access must not infringe on anyone else's rights and freedoms.

Right to Rectification

The Right to Rectification[18] is directly related to the OECD principle of "data accuracy."

Should a data subject become aware that the personal data related to them is inaccurate, they have the right to request that this be corrected.

A data controller faced with such a request must respond within one month from receipt, and must inform recipients of that data (if any) about the rectification.

Right to Erasure (the Right To Be Forgotten)

The Eight to Erasure[19]—more commonly known to as "the Right to be Forgotten"—is not an absolute right. The data subject has the right to request that personal data be erased if one of the following circumstances apply:

- The data subject has withdrawn consent.

- Personal data is no longer necessary for the purposes it was collected for.

---

16 GDPR Article 15
17 Should the data subject exercise this right more than once, the controller is entitled to decide to charge a reasonable fee for providing subsequent copies.
18 GDPR Article 16
19 GDPR Article 16

- The data subject objects to processing (presuming that there are no overriding legitimate grounds to continue such processing).

- The personal data has been unlawfully processed.

- The personal data must be erased on the basis of compliance with a legal obligation.

- The personal data is processed in relation to the offer of information society services to a child.

This is a right that gained significant popularity in 2014 with the Google Spain case we previously mentioned.[20] Many hailed this as a "new" right—however, this is a common misconception. This right had been prescribed in the Data Protection Directive from 1995, which is exactly how the Court of Justice of the European Union was able to make the judgement it did in the Google Spain case.

Right to the Restriction of Processing

A data subject has the right to obtain a Restriction of Processing[21] from the data controller if:

- The data subject contests the accuracy of the personal data; during this time the controller gets an opportunity to verify the accuracy.

- The processing is unlawful and the data subject opposes the erasure of the personal data and requests the restriction of its use instead.

- The controller no longer needs the personal data for the purposes of the processing, but it is required by the data subject for the establishment, exercise or defense of legal claims.

- The data subject has objected to processing for the performance of a public task or for legitimate interest.[22] (If in the latter case, the controller has to consider whether their legitimate grounds override those of the data subject.).

---

20 Google Inc. v Agencia Española de Protección de Datos, Mario Costeja González
21 GDPR Article 18
22 GDPR Article 6(f)

If the Right to Restriction is applicable, the controller can still store the personal data but must refrain from further processing and must make sure to only retain the personal data necessary for showing that the controller has restricted processing.

How to show that the controller has restricted processing is an interesting question, when one considers that even the storage of personal data is "processing." Emerging best practices suggest flagging records as "restricted processing," so that such flags can be seen by an operator (employee, contractor) when they view a record and do nothing more with the data. To actually implement access controls on a record level in a database or across other formats is impractical on a technical level, especially on legacy systems and applications.

Right to Data Portability

The thinking behind the Right to Data Portability is to protect an individual from "vendor lock-in." This right basically forces the service provider, e.g., an insurance company, to ensure that personal data is in a "portable" format that can be moved to another insurance provider.

The Right to Data Portability enables the data subject to receive their personal data in a structured, commonly used and machine-readable format and be able to transmit it to another controller without hindrance.

This right will be applicable:

- When processing was based on the data subject's consent or for the performance of a contract.

- When processing is carried out by automated means.

- To personal data obtained from the data subject.

The controller must respond to requests for data portability without undue delay and within one month from receipt.

There are some technical challenges in making this work in practice. Basically, specific industry sectors need to set up working groups to agree on a *de facto* standard to meet this requirement. There is no use in one organization trying to make this work without talking to other players in the same industry.

As global privacy expert Alexander Hanff has said: "Some most obvious ways forward for data portability would be for organizations to look at mapping JSON objects (or XML) for data relating to data subjects as both these formats are easily understood by third party systems."[23]

Right to Object

Data subjects have the Right to Object[24] when processing of their personal data is:

- Done for the purposes of direct marketing.

- Done for the purposes of scientific/historic research or statistics.

- Based on legitimate interest or the performance of a task in the public interest/exercise of official authority (including profiling).

Where the data subject objects to processing for direct marketing purposes, the personal data shall no longer be processed for such purposes.[25]

Rights relating to automated individual decision-making, including profiling

In order to get to an automated decision, profiling is a necessary. Profiling enables scalable big data analytics. Profiling is like placing an individual into a group. This profile information contains information about who we are and what we do. Profiling is performed both in private industry and by public sector authorities. In some cases, profiling by race, color, gender or creed, etc., can be used to discriminate against and ultimately cause harm to an individual. Once created, these profiles are attached to our identities and can influence decisions made about us. Each individual can be assigned hundreds of profiles. One example of the use of profiling by a company is to retain customer loyalty, i.e., by tailoring your buying experience specifically to you.

Data subjects have the right to not be subject to automated decision making without any human intervention, including profiling, that can produce legal or otherwise significant effect.

---

23 Source: Alexander Hanff CIPP/E, 2nd October 2017.
24 GDPR Article 21
25 GDPR Recital 70

This does not apply if:

a) Such decisions are necessary for the performance of a contract.

b) Such decisions are authorized by law (e.g. for the prevention of tax evasion).

c) Such decisions are based on a data subject's explicit consent.

In the case of (a) and (c) with regard to automated decision-making and profiling, a controller shall implement suitable measures to safeguard the data subject's rights, including offering the opportunity to obtain human intervention, express their point of view, and obtain a written reasoning for the decision with the possibility of challenging it.

Why a "legal basis for processing" is important (Article 6)

If you remember how the first principle of the GDPR talks about data processing being *lawful*? Well, here we touch on *a part of* what this actually means in practice.

What this means for the controller is that:

• Collection of personal data must be for a specific purpose.

• Processing requires a "legal basis."

According to the GDPR, processing activities must rest on one of six legal grounds. Without this, processing is, regardless of everything, illegal. Consequently, understanding on what legal grounds every single processing activity rests is of the utmost importance. Normally in the GDPR, personal data will be collected using the legal basis of consent or contract, and then data may be processed further based on one of the remaining legal bases, of which there are four. (At least this is how it will generally work in private sector.) Deviation from existing practices, citing legitimate interest, has been used quite liberally. This will be strongly discouraged in the GDPR, and is already causing quite a panic in the marketing professionals community.

Figure 5.Legal basis for processing (Article 6)

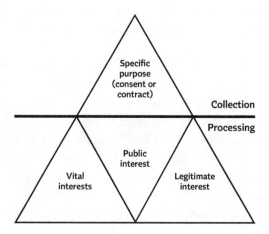

Processing shall be lawful only if at least one of the following applies[26]:

- *Consent* – the data subject has given consent to the processing of his or her personal data for one or more specific purposes.

- *Contract* – processing is necessary for the performance of a contract to which the data subject is party or in order to take steps at the request of the data subject prior to entering into a contract.

- *Legal obligation* - processing is necessary for compliance with a legal obligation to which the data controller is subject.

- *Vital interests* – processing is necessary in order to protect the vital interests of the data subject or of another natural person.

- *Public interest* – processing is necessary for the performance of a task carried out in the public interest or in the exercise of official authority vested in the controller.

- *Legitimate interest* – processing is necessary for the purposes of the legitimate interests pursued by the controller or by a third party, except where such interests are overridden by the interests of fundamental rights and freedoms of the data subject that require protection of personal data, in particular where the data subject is a child.

---

26 GDPR Article 6 (a)-(f)

Consent

Lawyers can spend whole days discussing consent and its implications, offering diverse legal interpretations that can drive you into a deep well of despair.

Consent is what you do, in the role as a data subject, before or upon the sharing of personal data. The legal entity or organization, whether public authority or private enterprise, must log this consent and be prepared to show it as evidence to the data protection authority on request.

Most non-privacy professionals think consent is the most frequently used legal ground for processing. But in reality, this is probably because it is the most over-used legal ground. In a lot of cases, organizations tend to throw in consent without thinking twice if it is really necessary. Remember: Consent is only one of the six legal bases for the processing of personal data.

A couple of common examples of cases in which you don't need to collect consent are:

- Employment administration. Most processing can be done on the basis of performance of the employment contract, compliance with legal obligation or the legitimate interest of the controller.

- Consumer purchasing on the Internet. Buying goods is entering a contract, and all processing necessary to deliver the product or service can rest on this legal ground.

Additional discussion of consent is provided in Appendix B: More on Consent.

Contract

You can probably think of loads of examples when you've signed a contract and the sharing of personal data is necessary. For example, as already mentioned, a contract is used as the legal grounds of processing data in your employment. When you purchase something—a house, a car, a service, or even a book online—you are a party in a contract. It is only the necessary processing in the performance of a contract to which the data subject is party[27] that falls under this legal ground, nothing

---

27 Processing necessary in order to take steps at the request of the data subject prior to entering into a contract is also legal according to this.

more. Just because there is no consent, it does not mean that the other seven principles do not apply; collection limitation, data quality, and purpose specification are legal requirements.

Legal obligation

In every industry, there are laws concerning the length of time that records pertaining to business operations need to be retained. In finance and banking, it's around 10-15 years. In clinical studies, you can expect research data to be stored in an archive for up to 25 years. This is why when you are conducting a privacy impact assessment under ISO 29100, there is "legal compliance" that does not purely relate to compliance with privacy laws, but also with other laws that could conflict with how long personal data is stored. In all cases, the compliance with legal obligations takes precedence over restrictions on the storage of personal data pertaining to use and minimization rules.

Vital interests of the data subject or of another natural person

This only applies in rare cases, such as in the hospital following an accident, whereby the life of the data subject is at risk and may not be in a position to provide consent.

Public interest

Well, this is what the Snowden disclosures were all about. Personal data has been collected indiscriminately, allegedly in the interests of public safety. Every country in the world has done this. Telecommunications equipment offers the technical capabilities, and each country has laws that basically give government authorities the power to eavesdrop on our analog and digital communications.

Legitimate interest

This is probably the most complicated legal basis. The legitimate interest of the controller must not outweigh the risk of harm to the data subject. This means in the situation whereby the five other legal grounds do not apply, processing is still permitted if it is in the legitimate interests of a controller (including of a controller to which the data may be disclosed) or of a third party, provided that those legitimate interests are not overridden by the interests of fundamental rights and freedoms of the data subject, in particular where the data subject is a child.

> **Recital 47:** *The legitimate interests of a controller, including those of a controller to which the personal data may be disclosed, or of a third party, may provide a legal basis for processing, provided that the interests or the fundamental rights and freedoms of the data subject are not overriding, taking into consideration the reasonable expectations of data subjects based on their relationship with the controller.*

In practice, this means companies will need to be careful in assessing if a legitimate interest exists by taking into account, among other things, the data subject's reasonable expectations at the time that processing takes place and the specific examples that the GDPR lists of when a legitimate interest may arise (which include, for example, processing of data for the purposes of preventing fraud or for direct marketing[28]).

Examples of legitimate interest (no brainers) are:

- Security measures such as log auditing or IT forensic investigations.

- The use of email address as authentication mechanisms to IT services.

- The use of personal data for security questions.

When conducting privacy impact assessments, you are bound to find cases in which legitimate interest has been used as the legal ground for processing. Legitimate interest is not new to the GDPR. The problem is that historically it has been used, in many cases, as the default legal option for processing; it is much easier than getting consent from the data subject. Your privacy impact assessment will need to assess these legal grounds, to ascertain if legitimate interest can really still be used.

---

28 It should be noted that marketing is only mentioned in a recital discussing legitimate interest. It has been debated among legal scholars what the intention by the law makers actually was with this. We believe it will not take long after May 2018 until marketing as a legitimate interest will be tested in courts.

A Risk-Based Approach to Privacy

The GDPR stipulates that "[i]n order to enhance compliance with this Regulation where processing operations are likely to result in a high risk to the rights and freedoms of natural persons, the controller should be responsible for the carrying-out of a data protection impact assessment to evaluate, in particular, the origin, nature, particularity and severity of that risk."

What is privacy risk?

Privacy risk is fundamentally simple; it is the "potential risk of harm to the data subject," period. But privacy risks can transform into corporate risks, and other risks can transform into privacy risks.

Privacy risk is fundamentally simple: It is the "potential risk of harm to the data subject." The problem is that even if you do enough to keep the supervisory authority happy, there is still potentially a risk of harm to the data subject—a consequence of the "privacy risk appetite" issue.

So here we go. An IT risk may not be a privacy risk, although an IT risk could equate to a privacy risk. (An IT risk may also present a risk to intellectual property (IP) and should have been managed following industry best practices such as the ISO 27001 gold standard in information security compliance.) If an IT risk is identified when conducting a privacy risk assessment[29], best practice is to hand it over to the CISO, as this risk is a potential liability to other aspects of the organization outside of privacy and GDPR compliance.

Now, the output of a DPIA could surface a corporate risk, e.g., brand damage, but a lot of other types of risks can also become corporate risks (such as insider dealing or lack of financial transparency). Furthermore, there can be other DPIAs happening in parallel, surfacing the same type of risks. If a corporate risk is found, it is smart to push it up for the corporate risk team to manage with a helicopter view of the accumulated risks.

What about a process risk? If there is no personal breach notification policy or any incident management process, then the industry best

---

29 A Data Protection Impact Assessment (DPIA) method to be covered in the following section.

practice standard in IT service management is not being followed. This can become a privacy risk. This is super interesting because we start to see how GDPR compliance can kick-start operational efficiencies that were previously lacking.

Now, privacy risk is a feed into the GRC (governance, risk, compliance) dashboard, also known as the ERM (Enterprise Risk Management) system. Either way, as a DPO you may be requested to sit in a steering committee for enterprise risk, and this can be both good ... and less good. On the good side is that you will get insight on risk decisions being made, including compromises that could present a privacy risk. Less good is that you could get dragged down with enormity of the risk landscape that diverts you from your primary role as DPO.

What is important is that the data subject and potential harms are specific to the scope of your role in data privacy. Everything else you can delegate or push up to the risk management team. It impacts the whole organization, and it is quite likely that you have enough on your plate without pulling that into the scope of your privacy program!

The "privacy risk appetite"

As the DPO you will need to make decisions on the risk appetite which you are willing to take on behalf of the data subject. Note that this is not the risk appetite of your organization. This refers to whether the collection and processing activities of your organization can cause harm to the data subject.

It could be that your organization is "GDPR mature" and the supervisory authority is satisfied that you have a positive privacy posture. You are following all the rules and ticking all the right boxes. However, all privacy risks have not been eliminated. Management has decided that to fully eliminate certain privacy risks is not commensurate with the benefits. It could be that the risk of harm to the data subject is so low, and the cost is so high to mitigate, that you as the DPO have decided to accept that risk on behalf of the data subject. It is, hence, a "privacy risk appetite."

The difference between "privacy risk appetite" and "risk appetite" is that the former is assumed on behalf of the data subject. The latter is being taken on behalf of the organization. Ultimately, if harm were to fall on the data subject, potential fall-out would be a corporate risk, such as brand damage. However, if the supervisory authority is satisfied that you have done all that was reasonable, apart from the associated inconvenience, risk of penalties would be low.

It is important to differentiate that a "privacy risk appetite" only becomes an option once you have got your organization to a positive privacy posture, i.e., "GDPR mature." It is only when you get here that you start to evaluate, "is it worthwhile to invest when the risk of harm is so incredibly low?" After all, when you get here, risk of penalties is also low.

Clearly it depends on each specific case, and this book will help you to understand why it is important to put on the shoes of the data subject—remember, we are all data subjects—when making these decisions.

Assessing privacy risk

Privacy risk should be assessed based on the likelihood and severity of the risk to the *rights and freedoms of the data subject*, taking into account the nature, scope, context and purposes of the processing. Risk should be evaluated on the basis of an objective assessment, by which it is established whether data processing operations involve a risk or a high risk.

Processing poses wide-ranging risks to the rights and freedoms of natural persons, of varying likelihood and severity, which in turn could lead to physical, material or non-material damage, including: discrimination, identity theft, financial loss, damage to the reputation, or any other significant economic or social disadvantage. Other risks may be that data subjects are deprived the right to exercise control over their personal data. More severe risks could be the disclosure of racial or ethnic origin, political opinions, religion or philosophical beliefs, trade-union membership, data concerning health, or criminal convictions. Another area of higher risk is where personal habits or characteristics are evaluated (in particular, analyzing or making predictions concerning performance at work, economic situation, health status, personal preferences or interests, reliability or behavior, location or movements) in order to create or use personal profiles or process personal data of vulnerable persons, particularly children. On a more general basis, risks are normally higher if the processing involves a large amount of personal data and affects a large number of data subjects.[30]

---

30 GDPR, Recital 75.

Corporate risk

There are potentially thousands of risks that can negatively impact an organization, and any of them can equate to a corporate risk. A common example is brand damage, in the event of a personal data breach that leads to personal data being lost or stolen. Such risks can stem from a combination of factors, including process, IT, human error, and much more as shown in Table 3. What this chart shows is that corporate risk can surface in the form of many guises.

Table 3. Corporate risk - guises of brand damage

Security	IT systems are not secure
Privileged User Access	Lacking policies concerning who can access IT systems and business applications
IT	Intrusion detection/prevention systems (IDS/IPS) were not implemented at all, or were not configured correctly
Training	• Personnel were not trained to take the output from security logs (sent to IDS/IPS) and interpret them in useful ways. • Employees haven't been made aware of what is personal data, what is processing, and why these definitions are important.
Privacy Policies	Lacking a privacy policy defining exactly "what is a personal data breach"
Process	Lacking an incident management process
Legal	Contracts with processors are lacking GDPR legal clauses
Communications	• The crisis and communications functions are not aligned with how to communicate externally in the event of a breach or incident. • Internal communications systems among employees (who are the "digital touchpoints" of an organization) are lacking.

Corporate risks can result from privacy risks not only through the imposition of monetary fines, but also through the disruption of business, e.g., if authorities demand that IT systems are shut down or processes are changed. Furthermore, any investigation conducted by an authority will require internal resources. Severe breaches coming to the public eye could also disrupt trust, followed by a decrease in sales. Lastly, for global companies, an investigation by an authority in one country could trigger another investigation by officials in another country.

There are hundreds of books on the market written by risk experts covering the calculation and management of enterprise risk. When you are looking at corporate risk with your "privacy spectacles" on, you keep track of enforcement and local legislation. Some resources you can use to make this easier are:

- The Global Privacy Enforcement Report released on a yearly basis by Data Guidance.[31]

- Some law firms also have examples of enforcement, such as Linklaters.[32]

From here, you can create your own enterprise risk heat map in the countries where you operate, by adding other metrics, i.e., number of local customers (data subjects), types of processing, etc.

Data Protection Impact Assessment (DPIA)

The target of **a privacy risk assessment is on personal data *not* IT systems.** DPIAs scoped around IT systems and/or IT departments are doomed to failure, because you need to first document from a business process the personal data flows running across the concerned IT systems which can make scope grow larger than anticipated at onset!

Outside of the EU, a privacy impact assessment (PIA) method is the most widely known method to identify and help reduce privacy risk on personal data processing activities. The data protection impact assessment referred to within the GDPR is a specific type of PIA that comes with unique legal obligations.

GDPR DPIA criteria

Article 35(7) stipulates that a DPIA should contain the following:

- A systematic description of the processing.

- Assessment of necessity and proportionality.

- Management of risks to the rights and freedoms of data subjects with involvement of interested parties.

---

31 www.dataguidance.com.
32 https://clientsites.linklaters.com/clients/dataprotected/Pages/Index.aspx.

In April, 2017 the Working Party 29 provided recommendations on what a data protection impact assessment should look like. The model provided in this book is aligned to these recommendations. What you can do is take this and other models on the market today and adapt to your business.

Regardless of the model you choose, what needs to be done is:

- Conduct DPIAs on existing data collection and processing activities that present a risk of harm to an individual.

- Implement a DPIA trigger within existing business processes that initiate the collection and or processing of personal data.

Figure 6. Data Protection Impact Assessment (DPIA)

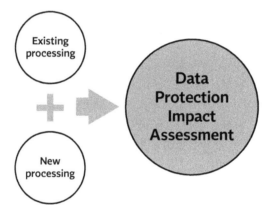

Getting started with a DPIA

If you have documented business flows, the time to complete a DPIA can be almost halved as personal data flows can be super-imposed onto the business flows if they are of good quality!

The data protection impact assessment in the GDPR is the recommended privacy risk-based approach that you must take in your organization. If you have documented business processes in your organization, you can start here. This means that you have documented swim-lanes of how a business process flows across your organization.

You may even have conducted Business Impact Assessments (BIA), which give you a matrix view of the business flow across systems and applications.

We have earlier recommended that when collecting evidence of your data processing activities, you send out a short 5-10 question questionnaire to the data-asset owner to get a quick response on high-risk assets early in the process, which should trigger the DPIA process.

The DPIA starts with an assessment of the data asset if there is no business process defined. You can expect a DPIA on personal data that is not documented within a business process to take 6-8 weeks. If a business process is defined and business flows documented with BIA output, it shouldn't take longer than 2-4 weeks, but clearly this is dependent upon the timeliness and quality of the flows and BIA.

> Data asset is the term used to describe the scope on a category of personal data to conduct a DPIA if there is no documented business process. For example, the personal data collected and stored in the payroll system could be called a data asset or the payroll business process.

A data asset contains the metadata of the actual personal data being collected. The process is a documentation of the data asset from the time of collection to when it is securely destroyed. The output are the data flows from collection through to destruction, accountability boundaries of the controllers/processors, and potential harm to the data subject[33] associated with the collection and processing of personal data, along with recommended remediation measures. What this means in summary, is the data asset is the input along with how it is collected and/or processed, the output is the documented data flows, accountable parties and risks.

Figure 7. Inputs/Outputs - Privacy Impact Assessment

---

33 The output of risks pertaining to the "potential harm to data-subject" are the identified risks.

When you dive you must to come up for air. Remember to do this at the stop gates **when conducting a DPIA**, and **take this breath of air with your sponsor**, to check you are on track.

The Agile 7-Step DPIA

There is no industry standard of best practice when conducting a DPIA, outside of the recommendations from the WP 29 at the writing of this book. The process provided here was devised by extracting the golden nuggets from PIA guidelines currently available around the world.[34] These guidelines are long documents, and our method has extracted the commonalities which you can take and adapt to your organization. This method has been tested and refined on: cloud services in both private and public sector, HR processes, CRM process, health care application, clinical trials, student registration, student learning processes, and more.

There are within the process stop-gates at steps two, four and five. This is where you take a sanity check, and are urged to take meetings with your sponsor to present your findings, before moving on. This is part of the Agile method, to ensure you are aligned within the context of the DPIA project.

Figure 8. 7-step Agile DPIA

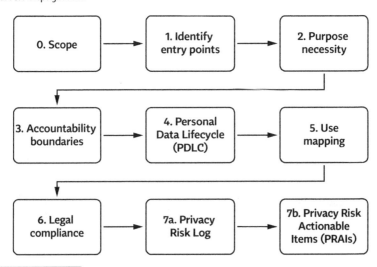

34 ICO in UK, Canada, Victoria (Australia) and U.S.

The process follows roughly an Agile approach in that the quality of input at each step leads into the next, which can trigger revisiting the former step as new facts emerge. This approach builds a quality process into your DPIA. It does mean that you will be continually revisiting previous steps as your DPIA scope refines itself into a lean and clean beast.

To say that it is seven steps is not entirely true; it is in fact eight steps, starting with a scoping step, the zero point. It is zero because it will provide the guiding framework for the PIA. You will return here over and over as new facts surface, which will guide you into a refined scope until you achieve perfection, with a list of Privacy Risk Actionable Items (PRAIs) by step 7.

Step 7 has two parts—(a) and (b)—(a) is initiated at Step 1 as it is the risks that you log during the process, and (b) comprises the output of the DPIA.

Step 0 – Scope

Where do you start? You are requested to conduct a privacy impact assessment on a system, and it all seems pretty straightforward, or is it?

Before you scope the project, questions you should be asking are:

How many data assets are contained within this system?

A privacy impact assessment should be done on personal data contained within a business process, or on a data asset (if there are no business flows defined), but definitely not on a system. For the first DPIA, you need to plan for at least eight calendar weeks until delivery of the Privacy Risk Actionable Items (PRAIs).

What this means is that if you are conducting a PIA on CRM data, the data asset will be personal data collected and processed for the purpose of assisting sales. This is a single DPIA, potentially with multiple data sets if the client purchases third-party personal data.

Each data asset will most likely have multiple collection points, and this should not cause confusion. Take the case of a wearable connected to a telecommunications network, which logs your sporting activities. Three collection points are mentioned below, but clearly there are many more.

- Global Positioning Services (GPS) data, which runs over telecommunications networks and is stored on their servers.

- Location Based Services (LBS) data which is stored on servers hosted by the controller (from whom the user purchased the wearable).

- A website where the user registers their device.

What other legal regulations are being followed?

The answer to this question can save you and your organization or client significant effort, especially if it is strongly regulated. Sectors that are strongly regulated include health care, finance and banking. If you are conducting a DPIA in any sector that is strongly regulated, we recommend that you get a subject-matter expert on your DPIA team.

You need to specify as a prerequisite the ability to have unhindered access to the owner of the business process. Just as with any project, you also need to have a Single Point of Contact (SPOC) through which you are able to escalate issues should that become necessary.

Step 1 – Identify entry points

The entry points, from the moment personal data leaves the data subject until it arrives—figuratively speaking—onto the lap of the controller, are documented here. It is a data flow and it is here you will start to log risks associated with the collection of personal data, and intermediaries between the collection point and the controller. You will need a specialist tool to create the data flows, and some knowledge of Unified Modelling Language (UML).

Figure 9. DPIA - Step 1 Identify entry points

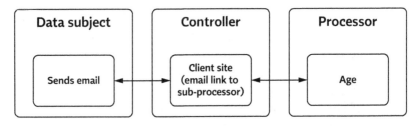

You should not document any more than what is defined within the scope of step 0 (however much you are tempted). If you continue with the flows at this early stage you could be wasting your time. For instance, what happens if:

- You get a STOP at Step 2?

- Your beautiful data-flows, through to backup media, are quite unnecessary when you realise that the IT environment is outsourced at Step 3, which means privacy risks are managed with legal contracts?

There are two parts to this step:

A. Documentation on the collection specifics at the data collection point

Questions which you can ask are:

- Is personal data acquired by first party or third party, or is it repurposed, i.e., is it a direct or indirect collection?

- Is the data subject active or passive in the collection?

- Does it include special categories of data?

- What are the personal data metadata attributes?

- Are there any intermediaries, i.e., processors between the point of data collection and the controller?

B. Data flows

Be aware that the data collection point may not be the data subject. For example, if personal data is collected for another purpose, such as the treatment of a patient, the collection point could be their historical medical records. This means personal data has been repurposed. There is no need to have a data flow from the actual collection of personal data, but only from the point of personal data repurposing, which is a form of indirect collection.

The data flows should diagrammatically represent the flow of personal data from the moment it is collected from the source—for example, data subject—until the controller (i.e. your client) has received it, nothing more. Why no more? Because you do not want to document the complete data flow at this phase, in case you find a purpose mismatch at Step 2, which means that no purpose is found for the collection and processing.

Step 2 – Purpose necessity

Stop-gate purpose mismatch

One of the most important stop-gates is this one, because you may just stop the DPIA, if you find there is no specific purpose for the collection of personal data (purpose mismatch). There is, hence, no need to continue, except for the purpose of a data discovery exercise within the scope of the DPIA. This is followed by the removal of all data entry points, all data in motion and at rest within the scope of the PIA.

You may wonder, why bother with any data flow before Step 2? It is useful to have sufficient information on the data asset to be able to hand over a purpose mismatch, if necessary, to the privacy program level in order for them to be able to easily find any dependences and remove all traces of such data collection and processing across the organization. This may require further data discovery, but at least with Step 1 and 2 together there is enough contextual data to make a decision, should a purpose mismatch be identified.

Privacy notice mismatch

If the purpose of collection and/or processing is affirmative, it is now the time to check that this purpose is communicated to the data subject in some form to align with the OECD Openness Principle. This could be in a privacy notice, information notice, etc. Any privacy notice mismatch must be appended to the risk log.

Refine scope by bringing all actors into the accountability matrix. The picture grows, but also refines as you place out-of-scope parameters within the matrix. **Out of scope of the DPIA does not mean out of scope for associated risks!**

Step 3 – Accountability boundaries

At this step, you refine scope by bringing all actors into the accountability matrix. The picture grows, but also refines as you place out-of-scope parameters within the matrix. Note that even the out-of-scope aspects present risks to the controller that need to be managed in some way.

If you are requested to conduct a DPIA but your sponsor does not have sufficient budget, you could offer to conduct a mini-DPIA, i.e., through Step 3. This will give you enough information to create a business case to raise additional budget for a complete assessment. This is because once you've completed this step, the risks begin to take form in your risk log (Step 7a).

Where do the accountability boundaries lie? In Step 3 you document all boundaries, even those that are out of scope of the actual PIA. The best way is to create a table (see the example below, which gives a full picture of accountability boundaries for a PIA conducted on personal data stored in the CRM system for a fictional company, Top Learning Books). If in doubt on whether to include an accountable party and their role, opt to include and place them out of scope. This table will give you a complete picture of why you made specific decisions later.

Top Learning Books purchases their CRM system as a cloud service and purchases personal data to be used in that system from CRM Quality Leads. What this means is that Top Learning Books is buying personal data from CRM Quality Leads, which is purchased as a service. It is CRM Quality Leads that is defining the purpose for the collection of personal data, which is then sold as a service.

As part of this service, CRM Quality Leads delete personal data stored in the CRM system when consent is retracted by the data subject. The joint-controllership could look a little as shown in Table 1: Joint Controllership.

Table 4. Joint Controllership

Accountable parties	Role	In DPIA Scope?	Contextual information
CRM Quality Leads	J-Controller	No	Sales leads (personal data) sold as service. Data subject deleted when consent retracted.
Top Learning Books	J-Controller	Yes	Append personal data to CRM

Sales executives in Top Learning Books append personal data, such as meeting and miscellaneous notes, to the purchased data. What this means is that for each lead, such as name of the head of a department of a school, part of the record is collected and maintained by CRM Quality Leads and another part is appended by Top Learning Books. This makes

Top Learning Books a joint controller together with CRM Quality Leads.

So, this gets interesting, because even though personal data collected by CRM Quality Leads is out of scope of the DPIA, the joint controllership starts to surface a potential risk. Top Learning Books needs to ensure that GDPR rules are followed on all third party data purchased and maintained by CRM Quality Leads, and the question that needs to be answered concerns the consent of individuals whose personal data is contained within the CRM system. We know that the data subject provided consent to CRM Quality Leads, but does this consent extend to personal data appended by Top Learning Books?

Your job is not to conduct a DPIA on personal data purchased from CRM Leads, but to get the legal teams of respective parties talking to each other to ensure GDPR rules are being followed by both parties. If not, then some decisions need to be made on how to manage the associated risks.

Step 4 – Personal data lifecycle (PDLC)

It is here that you pick up the data flows you created in Step 1 and finish them. The data asset you are assessing is starting to develop certain characteristics. It is at Step 4 that you finish assembling this puzzle, and it will give you what you need to complete the use mapping (Step 5).

Figure 10. Adapted from 'The Data Lifecycle' (Introduction to IT Privacy, Travis Breaux, CIPT)

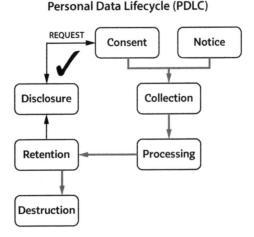

Personal Data Lifecycle (PDLC)

You have the data flows from the moment of collection, now you will extend the flows to the point at which the personal data is destructed. If your IT environment is outsourced, or you are using cloud services, you would not need to extend your personal data flows to the backup media; however, you will need to ensure that the correct data processing agreement is in place to ensure the processor is following industry best practices pertaining to the security and integrity of personal data. That is, they are following industry standards for privileged user access (PUA), secure techniques on the use of hardware encryption, destruction of hardware media, backup tape rotation, etc.

All personal data collected and/or processed must have an "end of life" defined and this should be included in the personal data inventory.

As you progress through the flows you will find surprises. There *must* be for each single flow (and there could be many):

- A direct correlation of personal data use to the specific purpose for collection.

- A legal basis for processes as defined in Article 6.

If your data flow is showing personal data copied to a document management system the organization is using, there is no end of life on the data, and neither of the two above criteria fit, you will probably have found a use mismatch.

Every swim-lane in your data flow can represent an accountable party as defined in Step 3. Now comes another important stop-gate in the DPIA process. You will schedule several meetings with your sponsor and the business process owner, to show your findings graphically. From here you may find:

- Version 1 and even maybe Version 2 of the data flows will be wrong, and it's back to the drawing board—this is normal if you are in a new environment.

- You confirm what your sponsor suspected—the reason why you had been assigned to conduct a DPIA.

- You surprise your client with findings that are unexpected (this is almost a guarantee!).

Step 4 is the most rewarding place to be in the privacy impact assessment. If you are gifted with the skills to simplify complex findings, you will have a simple data flow graphic representing the lifecycle of the data asset. You will have pulled out the gold nuggets from the mess you probably started with. Your risk log will get busy now, and if you did it really well, your hard work is already rewarding you with clear, shining path forward.

Step 5 – Use mapping

The use of personal data must be strictly aligned to the specific purpose and/or the legal basis for processing as defined in the GDPR Article 6, "Legal basis for processing." Without this, processing is illegal. Consequently, understanding on what legal grounds every single processing activity rests is of the utmost importance.

The use mapping is easy now, and you may even have completed it while working on the data flows. At this stage, you would have identified issues wherein the use of personal data is not aligned to the stated purpose for collection.

Step 6 – Compliance check

When you get to Step 6 you are basically filling in the holes on compliance with GDPR, along with any alignment with specific laws and regulations such as those found in banking and finance, health care or pharmaceuticals. This should be purely a tick-box exercise.

Step 7 – Privacy risks

Privacy Risk log

What should be mentioned now is that you are, during these seven steps, compiling a log of risks, which is finalized in Step 7. Each step will surface risks, and these are captured in the Risk Log.

Notation of these risks should be ongoing during the life of the project so you are able to backtrack and understand why certain risks never evolved into Privacy Risk Actionable Items (PRAIs). It is important that you have documentation of why you have discarded, or not taken action on, certain risks.

Privacy Risk Actionable Items (PRAIs)

This is the deliverable you will hand over to your client or sponsor. It refers to "actionable items" because it should be easy for your sponsor to identify specific actions to take toward mitigate these risks, for example, generating a business case for funding for a new project.

A privacy risk will either present a potential risk of harm to the data subject or potential damage to the business (if the former, the latter is inevitable). You will need to organize the risks by those which are specifically privacy risks, versus those that are more corporate risks and therefore should be managed by the corporate risk management team. Your project cannot own risks that are out of your control. For example, privacy awareness is something that will need to be pushed up to the privacy program level and IT risks will be delegated to the CISO, so you can focus on specific risks such as the legal basis for processing, processor agreements, etc.

What follows is a privacy model you can use to give a value and characteristics to your PRAIs.

A Privacy Risk Model

A fundamental feature of all privacy risk methodologies is that they should measure the privacy impact in a consistent and repeatable way over time. Without this it will not be possible to prioritize all the risks that appear within an organization. This is important since experience tells us it is just too easy to run at the ball in front of us instead of doing things in a systematic way. The risk of getting distracted by the most recent issue or incident will require trust in the methodology by all stakeholders.

A privacy risk model must include at least the following components:

- Identification of processing activities that can cause harm to the individual.

- A method for assigning probability.

- A method for assigning severity.

- Knowledge of mitigating actions available and the resources needed for implementing these actions.

With the first three components, you can start assessing the risks and get a heat map of all risks. With the fourth element in place, you can then start prioritizing among the mitigating actions and allocating resources. Once this model is complete, you should consider how to control the risk: transfer, accept or treat.

Transfer Risk

Different forms of insurance are a common way of transferring risks. Cyber insurances have exploded the last century. Recently we have seen that they could include data privacy elements. It is our anticipation this will become more common. But whether this actually works to successfully mitigate risks to the individual is still unclear.

Accept Risk

Traditionally, accepting risk is intrinsically linked to "risk appetite." Risk appetite, as you recall, is the amount of risk considered acceptable if the costs and/or efforts required to eliminate the risk completely are not economically feasible. In privacy, the potential harm to the individual is key. To assess risk appetite demands you to take the position of every single data subject, or at least estimate an average risk appetite among data subjects. In some circumstances, it can be argued that even without action to mitigate or reduce a risk, the benefits for the individual are greater than the risk of harm.

Treat Risk

This is the most common approach to privacy risks. Treating a risk is a method of controlling it through actions that reduce the likelihood of the risk occurring, or acting to minimize its impact before or after it has occurred. This could include stopping collection of a specific type of sensitive personal data if not strictly necessary. If possible without affecting the business, removing the risk should be the first option considered.

Implementation of controls

When the privacy risk assessment is finalized you should have a list of mitigating activities with prioritizations. However hard this exercise has been, the implementation phase is often twice as hard, in part due to allocation of resources. This phase could also include changes to the organization and/or processes.

Challenges, changes and continuous risk assessment

A privacy risk assessment should, as far as possible, anticipate risks throughout the information lifecycle. This will probably be a cross-organizational challenge since data collection, use and destruction processes are likely handled by different departments. We suggest you use the Agile 7-Step PIA model we have described.

It is important to monitor the effect of the mitigating actions that have been taken over time.

At the same time, an organization needs to keep up with both internal and external changes that could affect the risk in either of its components, i.e., likelihood and severity. Your privacy risk assessment should specify how often risks and effectiveness of treatment will be reviewed.

Privacy Risk Impact

The privacy risk is a function of the severity and likelihood of a processing activity causing negative impact on a data subject. Thus, the risk model should answer the question: "What is the nature, likelihood and consequence of the risk?"[35] Severity and likelihood can refer to:

- Severity: What is the magnitude of the negative effect on the individual? Consider the type of information, number of data subjects affected, etc.

- Likelihood: What is the probability a risk will materialize? The likelihood should be evaluated as per a typical individual in the data set.

Data Protection by Design (DPbD) as a Default

Data Protection by Design (DPbD) as a Default is not restricted to technology. The GDPR stipulates that DPbD must be the default operational mode at every level of your organization!

- What the General Data Protection Regulation (GDPR) means to businesses after 25th May 2018.

- What data protection by design (DPbD) as a default means in practice.

- DPbD in business processes.

- DPbD in technology.

- The privacy intelligence component

---

35 Privacy risk and opportunity identification, p.5, https://www.ict.govt.nz/assets/ GCPO/Privacy-risk-and-opportunity-identification.pdf

DPbD as a Default in practice

Data Protection by Design (DPbD) is *not* restricted to IT. Secure software development is necessary in order to have privacy in software and application development, but DPbD is much more. DPbD is about embedding privacy into business processes as well as the development lifecycle of any new product or application, and DPbD should become the default mode of operation in all of your business processes and IT systems after May 25, 2018. This will require the insertion of DPbD decision points into almost every business function across every organization.

In fact, a data protection impact assessment (DPIA) is an example of privacy by design in business processes. For example, a DPIA should be triggered automatically upon a new marketing activity that involves the collection of personal data—every time a new webpage is created with a form to collect an email address, or a new type of cookie is dropped onto a user's device.

Let us take the procurement function as an example. There needs to be, embedded into the procurement process, a privacy decision point: Will personal data be processed?

> **DPbD decision point to be added into procurement process**
> Will there be personal information collected and/or processed in the service or technology?

An affirmative response to this question should trigger a privacy risk decision concerning the purchase as shown in Figure 11.

Figure 11. DPbD as a Default - Procurement process example

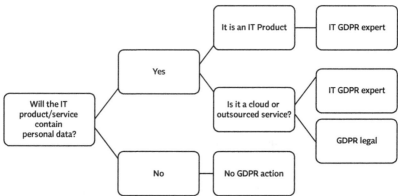

> The second GDPR decision point should trigger GDPR experts from the IT and legal fields (sometimes both) to serve as influencers into the purchasing choices.

With privacy as a key component of the procurement function, it is important to pull in IT and security experts. They need to be trained on the seven Privacy by Design (PbD) principles[36] and what they mean in practice.

That could translate into:

- Ensuring firewalls are properly configured.

- Implementing user access control management.

- Performing regular software updates.

- Employing real-time protection through anti-virus, anti-malware and anti-spyware software.

- Encryption of all portable devices ensuring appropriate protection.

- Encryption of personal data in transit by using suitable encryption solutions.

- Architecture in line with Privacy by Design (PbD).

Privacy by Design (PbD)

The seven PbD principles[37] were created in the 1990s to encourage more user-centric privacy thinking in all product and service development starting at the design phase. The seven principles (which have significant overlap with the OECD privacy principles) are:

- Proactive not reactive: preventative not remedial.

- Privacy as the default setting.

- Privacy embedded into design.

---

36 Ann Cavoukian, Ph.D (2009). Privacy by Design: The 7 Foundational Principles. https://datatilsynet.no/globalassets/global/english/7foundationalprinciples_anncavoukian.pdf (last accessed 4 January 2017)
37 The 7 PbD Principles were created by the former Information and Privacy Commissioner of Ontario, Canada, Dr. Ann Cavoukian, back in the 1990s, and have since been translated into 31 languages.

- Full functionality: positive-sum, not zero-sum.

- End-to-end Security: full lifecycle protection.

- Visibility and transparency: keep it open.

- Respect for user privacy: keep it user-centric.

Proactive not reactive; preventative not remedial

The Privacy by Design (PbD) approach is characterized by proactive rather than reactive measures. It anticipates and prevents privacy invasive events before they happen. PbD does not wait for privacy risks to materialize, nor does it offer remedies for resolving privacy infractions once they have occurred—it aims to prevent them from occurring. In short, Privacy by Design comes before-the-fact, not after.

You have processes today in your working environment that can be designed to promote proactive and/or preventative approaches. The use of incident reporting to recognize and resolve recurring issues is an example of being both proactive and preventative.

An effective breach notification process cannot prevent a breach, but it is proactive. And it could be preventative in terms of minimizing potential damage both to the data subject and the organization, after the fact.

Undergoing a DPIA is another example of a proactive approach to privacy, assessing—even before personal data is collected—if collection is really necessary, what is the purpose, and what are the associated risks. This is is a risk-based approach to privacy.

Privacy as the default setting

We can all be certain of one thing —the default rules! Privacy by Design seeks to deliver the maximum degree of privacy by ensuring that personal data are automatically protected in any given IT system or business practice. If an individual does nothing, their privacy still remains intact. No action is required on the part of the individual to protect their privacy—it is built into the system, by default.

In the GDPR, data protection by design should be implemented as a default across your organization, and in every product and/or service you offer to your customers.

Do you have a favorite social media account, where you share photos and life experiences with friends and families online? Have you ever looked at the privacy settings? These services normally do have some form of privacy controls built into the design, but they have not been enabled by default. You as the user must change the settings.

Privacy as a default means the settings should be, by default, switched on to protect user privacy. So, in the example provided here, if you decide to share a photo, by default, it should share with only yourself, unless you choose to share with others.

If you have made such changes to your default settings in order to protect your privacy, have you ever wondered why these settings are not, by default, set to protect?

Privacy embedded into design

Privacy by Design is embedded into the design and architecture of IT systems and business practices. It is not bolted on as an add-on, after the fact. The result is that privacy becomes an essential component of the core functionality being delivered. Privacy is integral to the system, without diminishing functionality.

This is *not* the same as privacy as the default setting, although without having privacy embedded into the design it is not possible to have privacy as a default.

A good technical example is an email service that has a "self-destruct" mechanism after a message has been read. Or social media services that ensure the user has control over what they share and how. Embedded privacy is not possible if the architects have not thought about this when designing the product.

An example of privacy embedded within a business process is if a privacy impact assessment (PIA) is triggered when the collection and/or processing of personal data is identified as part of any new project.

Full functionality: positive-sum, not zero-sum

> Privacy by Design seeks to accommodate all legitimate interests
> and objectives in a positive-sum "win-win" manner, not through a
> dated, zero-sum approach, where unnecessary trade-offs are made.
> Privacy by Design avoids the pretence of false dichotomies, such as
> privacy vs. security, demonstrating that it is possible to have both.

Trade-offs are pretty easy to grasp for anyone working in IT. We are well
aware of the trade-offs pertaining to usability versus security; this is why
we have Single Sign-On products! This PbD principle is about privacy
trade-offs in the name of security, such as with the use of biometrics for
authentication. In order for biometrics to work there is no choice but
to collect and store biometric data of individuals to restrict access to
systems, buildings, etc. Sensitive data must be properly collected and
used to provide security. By respecting PbD principles, controllers can
ensure privacy of the individual is not forfeited in the name of security.
Hence, it is positive-sum, not zero-sum.

End-to-end security: Full lifecycle protection

> Privacy by Design, having been embedded into the system prior
> to the first element of information being collected, extends
> securely throughout the entire lifecycle of the data involved —
> strong security measures are essential to privacy, from start to
> finish. This ensures that all data are securely retained, and then
> securely destroyed at the end of the process, in a timely fashion.
> Thus, Privacy by Design ensures cradle to grave, secure lifecycle
> management of information, end-to-end.

In practice, this means that from the moment of personal data collection
through all subsequent processing, there must be complete lifecycle
protection as well as a secure "end-of-life" procedure. This pertains to
personal data that can be mirrored across multiple systems, as well as
near-line, offline and the backup storage systems. This consideration
needs to be aligned with business criticality and the disaster recovery
plan (DRP).

Visibility and transparency: Keep it open

> Privacy by Design seeks to assure all stakeholders that whatever
> the business practice or technology involved, it is in fact, operating
> according to the stated promises and objectives, subject to
> independent verification. Its component parts and operations
> remain visible and transparent, to users and providers alike.
> Remember, trust but verify.

A privacy notice giving information on the collection and processing
activities of the controller is an example of this principle.

Another example is if there is a breach, i.e., a system has become
vulnerable to an attack and/or personal data may have been stolen, a
breach notification process should embrace transparency. The breach
should not be hidden; rather, it should be reported immediately to IT
management, in order that appropriate stakeholders can be informed if
required.

Respect for user privacy: Keep it user-centric

> Above all, Privacy by Design requires architects and operators
> to keep the interests of the individual uppermost by offering
> such measures as strong privacy defaults, appropriate notice, and
> empowering user-friendly options. Keep it user-centric.

When assessing an app on a mobile device, you would be looking for
controls on the collection of personal data. By default, it should not
collect. There should be a privacy notice that can be easily seen with one
click. When a user shares content or information, it should, by default,
share using the minimization principle, i.e., share to the user, who can
choose to share to a wider audience. It should be easier to have strong
privacy defaults in the use of the application, than the inverse.

Data Protection by Design is requirement for organizations in the
GDPR. DPbD needs to be implemented across the whole organization.

The GDPR states that the data subject has the right to request what
data the controller is storing on them and much more. So, you need
to think from a "data-asset" lens (data-subject centric) rather than a

IT-centric lens. This places demands on personal data beyond purely protection and availability, as is required when protecting organization data, such as intellectual property (IP).

PbD mirrors the eight OECD privacy principles, although it takes privacy to another level. PbD is about quality, not merely doing the minimum. You can liken the thinking behind PbD to well respected approaches to quality management and software development, such as the ISO 9001 Quality Management System (QMS), and the Software Development Life Cycle (SDLC).

Learning Activity

For discussion in groups, and/or in GDPR discovery workshops.

#	The GDPR
1	Sam White rings; he is a client for Your Insurance AB and requests a copy of all personal data that has been collected on him. What is the first thing you would do? The request arrived four days ago, and the request is not straightforward; you find out that a key person is on vacation for the next three weeks, what do you do?
2	You have been tasked with creating an inventory of all personal data collected and processed in your organization. How would you start?
3	Tom Grey, a sales representative for a product vendor, contacts you to offer a GDPR product that is allegedly able to "discover" personal data by using some special discovery techniques his company has patented. Would you meet with Tom? If so, what questions would you ask?
4	You are Lead for the testing team at Best Testing AG. Your customers send you the test data that you use to test that a new application is working as it should. GDPR will soon be effective—would you place any special requirements on your customers?
5	ACME Ltd. is going to contract with some GDPR experts to help assess the company's privacy risks. What questions would you ask in order to make sure the experts are actually what they claim?

CHAPTER 3

Controller & Processor Liability

Controller or Processor?

Your organization probably comprises multiple legal entities. What is important to understand is that **your organization will be held liable for the actions of your subsidiaries** if they are deemed controllers.

Who is the controller?

Your organization probably comprises multiple legal entities. What is important to understand is that your organization will be held liable for the actions of your subsidiaries. What is even more important to consider is that you could be liable as a controller even if you think you are a processor.

It is the controller who defines purpose of personal data to be collected and processed. If you are trying to work out who plays what role when conducting a privacy risk assessment, you need to start here.

Consider a scenario wherein the head office purchases sales leads in a CRM system which is a cloud service, and your sales teams, which happen to be in other countries and autonomous in their operations, are appending to this data when they follow up on sales leads. Who is accountable, and who is the controller?

Is it:

a) The organization that sold you the personal data?

b) The head office that purchased the personal data and CRM as a cloud service on behalf of the subsidiaries?

c) Or is it the subsidiaries who are adding their own leads, and appending to purchased data?

These answers cannot be answered in this book, these are answered by the completion of a privacy risk assessment on the personal data in question.

You must remember that your organization will be held liable for the actions of your subsidiaries. What this means in practice is that you need to consider the following actions:

- Decide on a Lead Supervisory Authority (SA) for your organization. By doing this you can funnel all your requests through this one channel instead of using a separate SA for every subsidiary of your business in each EU jurisdiction.

- Create a Privacy (or Data Protection) Office that oversees the organization.

- Create privacy policies and procedures on how personal data should be collected and managed.

- Conduct privacy risk assessments to ascertain accountability boundaries, roles of parties and risks.

Joint controllership: How does this work in practice?

When two or more controllers together determine the purposes and means of processing, it is necessary for the joint controllers to create an agreement, determining their respective duties, to comply with the GDPR.

The agreement must be available to data subjects and needs to assign one point of contact for data subjects. Regardless of the allocation of responsibility set out in the contract, data subjects are entitled to enforce their rights against either controller, which means that each controller is individually and equally liable for noncompliance with the GDPR.

We strongly recommend against using joint controllership since it could create a risk of complicated and expensive disputes.

You could be liable as a controller even if you think you are a processor. As a processor, you must do only what you have been instructed by the controller, nothing more. **Even if you are a processor to your clients, you are a controller to your employees.**

Who is the processor?

The processor must do only what they are instructed, and this needs to be evidenced in writing by the controller. For example, if the processor plans to bring in a sub-processor they must request a written acceptance from the controller, because they will be sharing personal data with another party, which they are not permitted to do as processor. They can, of course, make decisions about how they will support the controller strictly within their role as defined by the controller. For example, if the processor is hosting a system for the controller, it can make upgrades to that system, improvements to the design and security, etc.

Remember that every processor to clients is a controller to its employees. Whether a legal entity is a controller and/or processor is not decided on an organizational basis, but on what personal data is being collected. If you have a marketing team, you are a controller on personal data collected for marketing purposes. However, if you deliver IT services for your clients, then you could also be a processor so long as you follow specific rules.

Clearly, being a processor is significantly less demanding than being a controller. So, if you are a processor it is in your interest to continue in that role; what follows are some guidelines for doing so.

The first, and most important, is that you as the processor must *not* act as a controller or outside the scope of authority granted by the controller. If you do this, the GDPR will treat you as a controller and consequently subject you to the same rules as a controller.

To be on the safe side, your duty as processor is to follow *strictly* the rules of controllers, including:

- Process data *only* as instructed by controllers.

- Implement and have evidence of technical and organizational measures to comply with the GDPR.

- Maintain records on all personal data processing carried out on behalf of the controller. These records should contain contact information for the processors (subcontractors) and also of the controller to which you are providing a service.

- Know what type of processing is carried out for each controller.

- Have information on cross-border transfers if applicable.

- Gather evidence of technical and organizational security measures implemented to protect the confidentiality, integrity and availability of personal data being stored and/or processed.

- Implement measures to securely destroy or return personal data to the controller once processing is complete.

Finally, there are restrictions on subcontracting in the GDPR for processors, who are prohibited from using another processor without prior permission from the controller. You as the processor need to have evidence that the controller has agreed to the use of subcontractors.

> **Controllers are liable for the damage caused to the data subject by processing their personal data.** That is why the controller needs to be careful on their choice of processor. **A processor is liable only when they have *not* done what they have been instructed to do.**

Who is liable?

Controllers are liable for the damage caused to the data subject by processing their personal data. That is why the controller needs to be careful the entity they choose as processor!

A processor, on the other hand, is liable only when they have *not* done what they have been instructed to do in the controller-processor legal agreement, or where they have "acted outside or contrary to lawful instructions of the controller," as the GDPR states. What this means in practice is that parties bringing claims against processors under the GDPR must prove an additional element apart from damage and general noncompliance, namely, that the processors have violated one of their specific legal duties or contractual obligations.

If it is shown that the controller and/or processor is non-compliant with the GDPR, a legal battle will ensue to apportion blame between the controller and processor. When the controller and processor are joined in the same judicial proceedings, liability for damages may be apportioned among them according to their respective responsibility for the resulting harm to data subjects.

During the summer of 2017, processors appeared to wake up and request help in getting a grip on their risks by performing a risk limitation exercise. This is because they do not want to be held liable due to the actions or inactions of a controller!

In order to have data protection by design as a default (**DPbD**) in your procurement process there should be added the question **"Will personal data be collected and/or processed in this product or service? Y/N?"** If the response is affirmative a privacy risk assessment should be triggered.

Supplier management

Once a upon a time the IT department was the only "supplier" of IT services (hardware and software) within an organization. This was long before Bring Your Own Device (BYOD), Software as a Service (SaaS) and Data Protection Impact Assessments (DPIA). As more and more IT services are moved from internal IT departments to cloud solutions, supplier management has become a priority in order to keep data protection in line with the legal requirements. The GDPR is no exception. According to Article 28, a "controller shall use only processors providing sufficient guarantees to implement appropriate technical and organizational measures in such a manner that processing will meet the requirements of this Regulation and ensure the protection of the rights of the data subject." In the same article, it is stipulated that the controller and processor must enter into a contract that is binding on the processor with regard to the controller. The contract must set out the subject matter and duration of the processing, the nature and purpose of the processing, the type of personal data and categories of data subjects and the obligations and rights of the controller. This contract is normally called a Data Processing Agreement (DPA).

If the processor is outside of the EU it is important to remember that one of the exceptions from the prohibition of transfer of the personal data outside of EU must be applicable. In the vendor case, the three most commonly used exceptions are a) the vendor is Privacy Shield certified, if the data is traveling to the United States, b) the contract includes EU Standard Contractual Clauses, or c) the vendor is processing personal data in a country with adequate data protection according to a decision by the EU Commission.

In order to meet the new requirements of governance and structure, a few things need to be kept in records regarding processors:

- A list of all processors including necessary information, for example:

  ○ Assessment of the protection of personal data.

  ○ Purpose of processing.

  ○ Location of processing.

  ○ Data Processing Agreement identification number.

- Data Processing Agreements.

- Personal data transfers outside of the EU (and the exception applicable).

Another side of supplier management is suppliers offering traditional software. The GDPR doesn't explicitly mention these as they are neither controllers nor processors. Still, controllers or processors using the software they provide must meet the requirements of Data Protection by Design and as a Default. It is equally important to contractually make sure such software is GDPR-compliant, otherwise the risk does not lie on the supplier but on the controller or processor using the software.

International transfer of personal data

One of the main objectives of the GDPR is to simplify the free flow of information. That may sound good, but in reality, a whole chapter in GDPR is dedicated to unpacking the transfer of personal data to third countries. Perhaps it's not that simple or free after all. A transfer to a third country is not allowed unless it is done under certain exceptions; the main ones are:

Adequacy decision by the Commission

According to this exception, transfer of personal data to a third country may take place if the European Commission has decided that the third country, a territory or one or more specified sectors within a third country in question, ensures an adequate level of protection. An updated list can be found on the Commission's web page.

Appropriate safeguards are provided

The appropriate safeguards must include enforceable data subject rights and effective legal remedies for data subjects to be valid. These safeguards may be provided by:

- A legally binding and enforceable instrument between public authorities or bodies (The EU-US Privacy Shield).

- Binding corporate rules.

- Standard data protection clauses adopted by the Commission.[1]

- Standard data protection clauses adopted by a supervisory authority and approved by the Commission.

- An approved code of conduct together with binding and enforceable commitments of the controller or processor in the third country to apply the appropriate safeguards, including as regards data subjects' rights.

- An approved certification mechanism together with binding and enforceable commitments of the controller or processor in the third country to apply the appropriate safeguards, including as regards data subjects' rights.

Derogations

The above exceptions will probably be the ones mostly used. But if you are in a position where none of them apply, there are some additional exceptions ("derogations" in GDPR language) for specific situations when the transfer can take place in the absence of an adequacy decision pursuant of appropriate safeguards. But these conditions should be used carefully and are as follows:[2]

1   The Commission's Standard Contractual Clauses (EU Model Clauses).
2   Article 49 (1) (g) is intentionally left out.

- The data subject has explicitly consented to the proposed transfer, after having been informed of the possible risks of such transfers due to the absence of an adequacy decision and appropriate safeguards.

- The transfer is necessary for the performance of a contract between the data subject and the controller or the implementation of pre-contractual measures taken at the data subject's request.

- The transfer is necessary for the conclusion or performance of a contract concluded in the interest of the data subject between the controller and another natural or legal person.

- The transfer is necessary for important reasons of public interest.

- The transfer is necessary for the establishment, exercise or defense of legal claims.

- The transfer is necessary in order to protect the vital interests of the data subject or of other persons, where the data subject is physically or legally incapable of giving consent.

U.S. and the Privacy Shield

Starting in the year 2000, transatlantic transfer of personal data was possible from the EU to an organization in the U.S. that was "self-certified," in that they adhere to seven principles included in the Safe Harbor agreement between the EU Commission and the U.S. Department of Commerce. All companies self-certified under the Safe Harbor scheme were deemed to have an adequate level of data protection. Until October 6, 2015, this was without a doubt the most important exception from the prohibition of transfer of personal data outside of the EU. On that day, the European Court of Justice invalidated the EU Commission's Safe Harbor Decision and in doing so, made all transfer of personal data relying on the Safe Harbor agreement illegal if none of the other mechanisms were in place. In order to fill the gap after Safe Harbor, the EU Commission and the U.S. government started to discuss a new agreement with a principle that would meet the requirement of data protection adequacy.

The EU-U.S. Privacy Shield adopted by the EU Commission on

July 12, 2016, is the current framework for transatlantic exchanges of personal data. To learn more about the Privacy Shield you can visit the official U.S. website, www.privacyshield.gov.

Personal data inventory

What the GDPR says

The GDPR stipulates that you must keep a register of *all* personal data-processing activities, and for this you need a type of asset register. According to Article 30, such a register (or "record" as GDPR calls it), should include some of the following obligatory information. But don't see this list as exhaustive. Your organization will probably need additional information. The minimum requirement is:

- The name and contact details of the controller and, where applicable, the joint controller, the controller's representative and the data protection officer.

- The purposes of the processing.

- A description of the categories of data subjects and of the categories of personal data.

- The categories of recipients to whom the personal data have been or will be disclosed including recipients in third countries.

- Where applicable, transfers of personal data to a third country, including the identification of that third country and if applicable the specific documentation proving appropriate safeguards.

- Where possible, the envisaged time limits for erasure of the different categories of data.

- A general description of the technical and organizational security measures.

Scoping your data discovery project

For the really large, complex organization where just this activity alone seems an impossible task, advice is to start with a "quick-and-dirty" inventory of all personal data as swiftly as possible. If you have assigned ownership to business processes, then at least you have owners of personal data. You can push out a 5-10 threshold questionnaire to owners in order to quickly surface high-risk personal data.

Examples of threshold questions could be:

- Does the business process contain personal data?

- Is there included sensitive data?

- What is the purpose for the collection of personal data?

- What is the quantity of personal data stored, for example, number of clients?

- Do you have the data available on any of your mobile devices?

- Do you know if the personal data is transferred or shared with a third party?

- Do the processing include profiling of individuals?

> Even though there are automated data discovery tools on the market you can forget them. **The personal data inventory requires manual effort, personal data cannot be fingerprinted**. Although AI may change this in the future!

Expect that the responses you receive will not be of good quality if you do not start on the "inside-out" component of your privacy program, which is the privacy awareness training.

Depending upon the size of your organization, this large project can get somewhat out of hand even if the scope definition is clear. That's because a significant amount of personal data that is collected and processed by an organization is invisible, hence the "unknown factor." One recommendation is that you split this into at least three or more projects, as follows:

1. Centralized business functions: Personal data stored in approved centralized business processes/functions that have assigned owners. This is low-hanging fruit because you have an assigned owner to the business function, who will be the personal data owner.

2. Departmental business functions: Personal data stored in approved business functions operating at a departmental/

country/regional level. As with the previous project, you should have a business owner for personal data.

3. Personal data that is collected and processed by departments and employees which are not approved business functions.

Project scoping and execution of (1) and (2) can happen top-down. Project (3) is dependent upon employee engagement, and privacy awareness activities.

By splitting this project into by what is "known" and what is "not-known" (i.e., invisible personal data processing activities) means you can get those green tick-boxes early in the data-discovery activity, and you won't be dragged down by Project (3) which will take some time and requires a different approach.

Is a special tool needed?

You may need to invest in a tool that gives you a view of personal data inventory, which ideally will deliver an exception reporting mechanism on high-risk personal data collection and whether a privacy impact assessment has been triggered and associated risks remediated.

Whether or not you need to invest in a tool is dependent upon factors such as:

- Number of employees.

- Number of clients.

- Number of partners.

- Complexity of category types collected.

- Special categories of data (sensitive personal data).

Let's say your business has five employees and you have developed a sporting app that collects special categories of data and has about 100,000 users. You may not need any tool outside of a spreadsheet to log categories of data collected and number of data subjects, even though sensitive data is one of the categories (Special in Table 5). This is because even though the service itself is privacy-invasive, the business model is not complex. It is a single product, offering a single service.

The table below also reflects the personal data you collect on your employees.

Table 5. Categories of data - Sporting App

Category of data	No. of employees	B2B	B2C	Misc.	Special Y/N
Employee data	5				HR data
Client data			100,000		
Marketing data					
CRM data					
Recruitment process				Applicants unknown	

You will, nonetheless, need to conduct a DPIA on personal data collected within the app and assignment on the app itself to ensure that the Privacy by Design principles have been followed in design and development processes. There also needs to be a trigger for a new DPIA if any changes in the collection or processing of personal data occur, e.g., integration of a heart-rate monitor into the app.

Consider, on the other hand, that your business has a more complex model including both B2C and B2B, with more than 2,000 employees. You have mature sales and marketing functions, which significantly increases the complexity. In the example below, client data is only 20,000 compared with the previous example of 100,000 but CRM data holds personal data of 50,000 leads, and 200,000 individuals' personal data is stored in marketing. The table offers a simplistic view; it is likely that personal data has been duplicated numerous times within marketing, via the use of different tools.

Table 6. Categories of data - complex example

Category of data	No. of employees	B2B	B2C	Misc.	Special Y/N
Employee data	200				HR data
Client data		40	20,000		
Marketing data			200,000		
CRM data		50,000			Meeting notes, freetext
Recruitment process				Applicants unknown	Sometimes in introduction letter

There are some good data-inventory products on the market specifically designed to fulfil this requirement. Automated means of data discovery are not recommended because they will only be able to "find" personal data that has a specific pattern. This work is a manual effort. Personal data can potentially be any data linked directly or indirectly to an individual. It would be very difficult to program this into any tool, although maybe in the future artificial intelligence (AI) will be able to do this.

Security of processing operations

This book doesn't intend to be an information security book; there are loads of books on the market already doing this. However, this section has been added to address how you may need to think differently about information security beyond what you are already doing by complying with the family ISO27x of information security standards.

Going beyond CIA

The information security model that forms the building blocks of your infosec program defines how you think about security. The traditional model of a confidentiality, integrity, availability (CIA) triad has been the *de facto* standard in information security for more than 30 years. It is the model referred to by security professionals globally and is still taught in universities today. However, the evolution of digital communications, the use of data analytics, and everything that has been addressed in the GDPR makes this model insufficient for the protection of personal data.

The Parkerian Hexad[3] does something to address this shortfall. It is a set of six atomic elements developed by Donn B. Parker in 1998. He was a bit ahead of his time as the model hasn't been widely implemented to replace CIA.

The first three elements of the model, if you have an infosec background, you will recognize from the CIA triad; the remaining three are new. This model has been adapted to a privacy context by referring to "personal data" rather than "data" and the addition of a seventh element called "resilience."

Confidentiality

Personal data must be protected from unauthorized access. This could be achieved with the use of encryption, or by restricting access. The GDPR states that personnel should be given the minimum access needed to do a task by default.

Integrity

The integrity of personal data must be protected from unauthorized modification.

Availability and Resilience

Personal data should be available when needed. Availability and resilience have been separated in the GDPR. Resilience is referring to aspects such as fall-over, backups, etc., availability is more to user availability, e.g. password reset function does not work so the application is not available.

Utility

This refers to the usefulness of data. A couple of examples: If an encryption key is lost, it ceases to be useful. Or, if personal data is anonymized in order to be used in a test environment, if it is anonymized to a state that it loses its utility—the data ceases to be useful.

Possession/Control

Even though the data subject will share their personal data with a controller, which means the controller has possession, the GDPR has given the data subject control. This element of the model separates possession from control, which is helpful when considering security in the context of privacy compliance.

---

3   (last accessed 18 January 2018, https://en.wikipedia.org/wiki/Parkerian_Hexad)

Authenticity

This refers to the assurance that a message, transaction, or other exchange of information is from the source it claims to be from. Authenticity involves proof of identity. In order to respond the right of access (right of the data subject), you need to prove that the individual is who they say they are beforehand.

"Personal Data Breach" Notification

A "personal data breach" needs to be treated separately from a normal "data breach." There is no legal requirement to report on a "data breach," but things change in the event of a personal data breach, with risk of penalties on non-compliance.

What is a personal data breach?

The requirement for personal data breach notification stipulates that the national data protection authority must be notified of a breach of security leading to the accidental or unlawful destruction, loss, alteration, unauthorized disclosure of, or access to, personal data transmitted, stored or otherwise processed. Notification shall be made without undue delay and, where feasible, not later than 72 hours after having become aware of the breach. If notification is not made within 72 hours, there must be good justification.

Under the GDPR, a **"personal data breach" is "a breach of security leading to the accidental or unlawful destruction, loss, alteration, unauthorized disclosure of, or access to, personal data** transmitted, stored or otherwise processed."

An exception to the supervisory authority notification requirement: Notice is *not* required if the personal data breach is unlikely to result in harm to the data subject.

When to press the alarm?

In order to meet the 72-hour personal data breach-notification window, you may be doing things a little differently. Your systems are reporting thousands of errors/incidents every week in their system logs. You may have an Intrusion Detection/Prevention System (IDS/IPS), which has done some intelligent correlation to an alarm dashboard. The challenge is knowing: 1) which applications/systems contain personal data, and 2) when to press the "personal data breach" alarm.

By now you should understand that it is important to store personal data separately from organizational data. This means you will be able to separate potential personal data breach alarms (72-hour notification window) from other organizational data in your dashboard.

Now say that you have ascertained that some anomaly has occurred in one or multiple systems/applications containing personal data. It is popping up in red on your dashboard. When do you know that a personal data breach has actually occurred? You may suspect a breach has occurred, but it could just be an anomaly. Normally, you'd just keep watching the logs, perhaps report a suspected security incident, and monitor to see how things develop over time, but with a potential personal data breach you do not have this luxury. You only have 72 hours.

What we recommend is that you document what type and quantity of anomalous behavior constitutes an affirmative breach, and what within your organization is a technical definition of a personal data breach. For example: There need to be three reported system anomalies on systems/applications containing personal data in order to trigger the breach notification process. (It may not be three; it could be five, or more, but the point here is to have a standard definition, even if it is not perfect.)

By having a clear definition, you can explain not only why you reported a personal data breach, but also why you did not, as the case may be. Evidence of an internal process trigger provide a justification as to why notification was *not* made to the supervisory authorities—even if, in hindsight, this decision turns out to have been wrong.

Communication to the authorities

If a personal data breach can be determined, all necessary information for notification needs to be collected. In addition to the name and contact details of the data protection officer (DPO) or other contact point where more information can be obtained, this will include the description of the:

- Nature of the personal data breach including where possible, the categories and approximate number of data subjects concerned and the categories and approximate number of data records concerned.

- Likely consequences of the personal data breach.

- Measures taken or proposed to be taken by the controller to address the personal data breach, including, where appropriate, how to mitigate its possible adverse effects.

An example of the process for notification to the authorities is shown in the flow below. Similar processes should be established for notification to data subjects. The processes for launching a privacy risk assessment to establish appropriate mitigating activities should be linked to this process (see Figure 12: Personal data breach notification process).

Communication to data subject

If the controller has determined that the personal data breach "is likely to result in a high risk to the rights and freedoms of individuals," they must also communicate information regarding the personal data breach to the affected data subjects, and this must be done "without undue delay." The GDPR provides exceptions to this additional requirement to notify data subjects in the following circumstances:

- The controller has "implemented appropriate technical and organizational protection measures" that "render the data unintelligible to any person who is not authorized to access it, such as encryption."

- The controller takes actions subsequent to the personal data breach to "ensure that the high risk for the rights and freedoms of data subjects" is unlikely to materialize.

- When notification to each data subject would "involve disproportionate effort," in which case alternative communication measures may be used.[4]

4   Rita Heimes (2016). Top 10 operational impacts of the GDPR: Part 1 – data security

Communicating a breach

A personal data breach has occurred and now the communication channels need to open. If the incident is not handled transparently, that not only breaks the GDPR's requirement for transparency in communications, but also has the potential to inflict damage to your brand.

Your communications team should be trained on internal and external communications in the event of a breach. They should be savvy enough to be able to describe what a personal data breach is, and to respond to questions that may come to them via diverse channels. How they communicate can be the deciding factor on how the news is received by your customers, business partners, and stakeholders within the national and/or global ecosystem.

---

and breach notification. The Privacy Advisor (last accessed 6 January 2017).

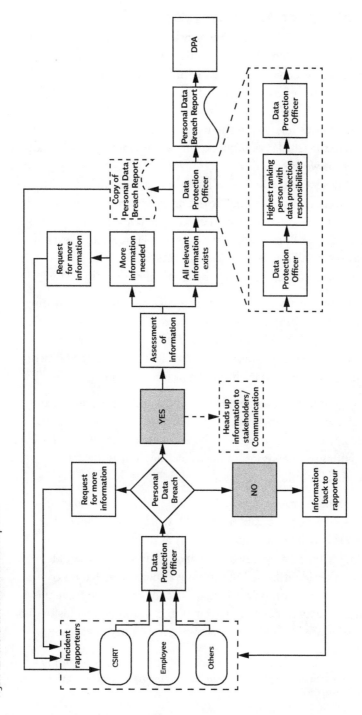

Figure 12. Personal data breach notification process

What about cookies and marketing?

The ePrivacy Directive, more popularly known as the "Cookie Directive", hooks into the Data Protection Directive, which means that it will not work once the Directive is replaced with the GDPR in 2018. It will be replaced by the ePrivacy Regulation, an initial draft of which was released by the European Commission in August 2017 and which a final draft of which was released in August 2017 and which is now making its way through the legislative process. This will impact how your marketing department is working today!

The ePrivacy Regulation looks like it will take a more holistic approach, treating any personal device as an extension of an individual, given how we live today in a world of social networking, Internet of Things, intelligent homes, etc. It may very well force a high level of privacy rules for all electronic communications.

An idea of its scope, according to the initial draft, follows:[5]

- The new privacy rules will apply to all organizations providing electronic communications services such as WhatsApp, Facebook Messenger and Skype. This will ensure that these popular services guarantee the same level of confidentiality of communications as traditional telecoms operators.

- Privacy must be guaranteed for communications content and metadata, e.g., time of a call and location. Metadata has a high privacy component and is to be anonymized or deleted if users did not give their consent for collection, unless the data is needed for billing.

- The cookie provision, which has resulted in an overload of consent requests for internet users, will be streamlined. The new rule will be more user-friendly as browser settings will provide for an easy way to accept or refuse tracking cookies and other identifiers. The proposal also clarifies that no consent is needed for non-privacy intrusive cookies that improve the internet experience (e.g., to remember shopping cart history) or cookies used by a website to count the number of visitors.

---

5   European Commission (2017). Proposal for ePrivacy Regulation. https://ec.europa.eu/digital-single-market/en/proposal-eprivacy-regulation (last accessed 14 January 2018).

- This proposal bans unsolicited electronic communications by emails, SMS and automated calling machines. Depending on national law, people will either be protected by default or be able to use a do-not-call list to avoid marketing phone calls. Marketing callers will need to display their phone number or use a special prefix that indicates a marketing call.

- Enforcement of the confidentiality rules in the Regulation will be the responsibility of data protection authorities, already in charge of the rules under the GDPR.

The conditions for consent in any revision of the ePrivacy Directive will derive from the GDPR. The two legal bases most commonly used today in the digital advertising sector are consent and legitimate interest. Under the ePrivacy Regulation, consent must follow GDPR rules, and the data subject must be able to choose what they consent to, e.g., it cannot be bundled with terms and conditions. The data subject should not be forced to consent to sharing personal data in order to access a service. It cannot be an "all or nothing" approach. The data subject must have choice.

Legitimate interest still can be relied upon as a legal basis to process personal data, but organizations will need to balance that justification with the rights and interests of the individual. The recitals in the GDPR specifically state that such legitimate interests include:[6]

- Where there is a relationship between the organization and the individual (e.g., subscription service).

- For internal administration purposes.

- For the prevention of fraud.

- Network security.

- Meeting legal obligations.

- Direct marketing.[7]

---

6 The Internet Advertising Bureau UK (2017). GDPR: A Briefing for the Digital Advertising Industry. https://iabuk.net/system/tdf/The%20EU%20General%20Data%20Protection%20Regulation%20%28GDPR%29_Online%20Version.pdf?file=1&type=node&id=28712 (last accessed 14 January 2018).

7 There is no definition of direct marketing in the GDPR and it is unclear how it might apply to many digital advertising at the time of writing this book

This is going to impact marketing team in a big way, if they have been citing legitimate interest almost as a default over other legal bases for processing (even though they should not). With the GDPR, legitimate interest (Article 6(f)) can no longer be used as the *de facto* choice of legal basis for processing; if it is cited, there needs to be solid grounds, with evidence. The ePrivacy Regulation[8] alone will be the subject of significant discussion—probably after the publication of this book!

Advice at this stage is just to make sure your marketing department is compliant with the ePrivacy Directive implemented at the time of publication of this book.

Some key tips are:

- Do not use legitimate interest as the *de facto* legal basis for processing.

- Ensure that the data subject has a choice not to share personal data.

- Opt-out is no longer an option, it must be opt-in.

- Before any campaign, trigger a mini DPIA!

Sanctions

Now we get to the nitty gritty. How much will it cost if your organization gets this wrong? In this section, we are going to look at the matter of fines and compensation.[9]

Ever since the first draft of the GDPR went public, discussions regarding the introduction of severe sanctions have been in the spotlight. Anyone with even the slightest interest in data protection has most certainly heard about fines of 20 million euro or four percent[10] of global turnover, whichever is highest. Fines like this could scare any company. But it is not only the fines that organizations should worry about. Beside the fines, the data subjects have a right to compensation. The actual monetary cost will thus be the fine plus compensation. And not to be forgotten is all the additional corrective powers the data protection authorities have.

8 https://ec.europa.eu/digital-single-market/en/proposal-eprivacy-regulation
9 Penalties are dealt with in the section on national derogations.
10 In the first draft from the Commission it was even higher, five percent of the global turnover.

Corrective powers

A data protection authority will probably use one of the other corrective powers[11] before imposing a fine, for example:

- To issue a warning if the intended processing operations are likely to infringe provisions of the regulation.

- To issue reprimands where processing operations have already infringed provisions of the regulation.

- To order compliance with the data subject's requests to exercise his or her rights.

- To order processing operations to be in compliance with the regulation.

- To order the rectification or erasure of personal data or restriction of processing.

- To order the suspension of data flows to a recipient in a third country or to an international organization.

For obvious reasons, an order for temporary or permanent restriction of processing can have severe effects on a business, as could an order to suspend data flows to a third country. Both business models and procedures and IT systems take time to change. If processing of personal data is at the center of your organization, such a decision by the authorities could have devastating effect, even putting you out of business.

Fines

First of all, it is important to note the GDPR only deals with administrative fines, not criminal fines. Being in breach of an obligation in the GDPR doesn't necessarily mean you have a criminal liability. Criminalization is up to each member state to decide on.[12] This means it will normally be a data protection authority that decides on fines. These penalties can be divided into two categories: high fines and very high fines, according to Article 83(5) and Article 83(6) respectively. In each of these, there's an enumeration of articles to specify if high or very high fines are applicable.

---

11 GDPR, Article 58(2).
12 See section on national derogations.

But before you start scaring every stakeholder in your organization, we should have a look at circumstances making things worse or better. As a general condition, all fines in the individual case must be *effective*, *proportionate* and *dissuasive*. The fines could be imposed in addition to, or instead of, other measures. Furthermore, it is stated in the regulation itself what the authority should consider when evaluating the level of fines:

- The nature, gravity and duration of the infringement, taking into account the nature scope or purpose of the processing concerned, as well as the number of data subjects affected and the level of damage suffered by them.

- The intentional or negligent character of the infringement.

- Actions taken to mitigate the damage suffered by data subjects.

- The technical and organizational measures implemented.

- Relevant previous infringements.

- Degree of cooperation with the supervisory authority, in order to remedy the infringement and mitigate the possible adverse effects of the infringement.

- Categories of personal data affected by the infringement.

- Manner in which the infringement became known to the supervisory authority, in particular whether, and if so to what extent, the controller or processor notified of the infringement.

- Compliance with previously ordered measures against the controller or processor regarding the same subject-matter.

- Adherence to approved codes of conduct pursuant or approved certification mechanisms.

- Any other aggravating or mitigating factor applicable to the circumstances of the case, such as financial benefits gained, or losses avoided, directly or indirectly, from the infringement.

Without question, intentional infringement is a very aggravating factor and even worse if it is done in order to reap financial gain. Worse still if it involves large amounts of "sensitive" personal data. Meanwhile, fines are only one side of the monetary sanction, with compensation being the other.

Compensation

Any person who has suffered material or non-material damage as a result of GDPR infringement shall have the right to receive compensation from the controller or processor for the damage suffered. Both the controller and the processor are liable for their own compliance with specific obligations directed to them. But the controller or processor shall be exempt from liability if it proves that they are not in any way responsible for the event giving rise to the damage. Furthermore, if a controller or processor has paid full compensation for the damage suffered, that controller or processor shall be entitled to claim back from the other controllers or processors involved in the same processing that part of the compensation corresponding to their part of responsibility for the damage.

Fines have been used as a whip to GDPR compliance since the draft came out in 2012. However, somewhat lost in this discussion are the corrective powers entitled to the authorities and the individual's right to compensation—especially the latter, which will probably play just as an important role as fines (maybe even more important). Imagine all data subjects in a customer database are entitled to compensation, and the compensation is 1,000 euro apiece. Companies with hundreds of thousands of customers or even millions of customers will then have to pay multi-millions or billions in compensation.

Another side of compensation claims will be the resources necessary to handle the litigation process.

Learning Activity

For discussion in groups.

#	Controller & Processor Liability
1	Learning Books AB has operations across 10 EU member states. Each of the subsidiaries uses the CRM, which is provided by the mother company based in Sweden. Each country is importing third party data that they have purchased in their country, which is appended to by the employees during the sales life cycle. As a privacy risk professional, what risks do you see in this setup?
2	You are holding a booth at a conference and the marketing team recommended holding a lottery to encourage visitors. Participants will be asked three questions; once they have provided contact and related organizational data, they receive a score, and if they got all three questions right, they will be included in the lottery. Would you advise marketing to approach this differently, and why?
3	You operate a call help center in the gaming sector (Gaming Help Malta Ltd.). You have many clients, to which you offer services via a chat dialog which pops up on their websites. Sometimes the call center receives a request for a player to be removed, because the customer has a gaming addiction problem. Gaming Help Malta Ltd. has initiated a "good gaming practice," which flags these players as "gaming addicts" and passes the information to their clients so that they will not contact the gamer again. Is Gaming Help Malta Ltd. a controller or processor in this scenario and what risks does the company need to address in whichever role they have?
4	One of your employees has lost a laptop in the airport which has job applications of five shortlisted individuals on his computer. Should you notify the supervisory authority?
5	What are the most critical components that need to be implemented, both in process and technology, in order to have an effective personal data breach notification strategy? Which industry standards could you leverage?

CHAPTER 4

The Privacy Program

Controller as Custodian

The data subject loans personal data to the controller in order to fulfil a specific purpose. Hence the role of the controller is as "trusted custodian" of personal data.

The "trusted custodian"

You don't need to be a legal expert to take the simply explained OECD privacy principles in this section as a basis for your organization to create a data protection system with rights and obligations which come together to form a coherent trust system. From here you can start to conceive of your organization could be seen as a trusted custodian of personal data.

In 2009, the concept of privacy was defined by the American Institute of Certified Public Accountants and the Canadian Institute of Chartered Accountants in Generally Accepted Privacy Principles (GAPP)[1] as "the rights and obligations of individuals and organizations with respect

---

1 GAPP is one of the most elaborated frameworks on Privacy so far. Together with the OECD principles it can form the base of almost any privacy program. It is also wider than just compliance with a specific law. GAPP was developed "to help management create an effective privacy program that addresses privacy risks and obligations, and business opportunities." Generally Accepted Privacy Principles, CPA and CA Practitioner Version, April 2009, p.8.

Hands-On Guide to GDPR Compliance

to the collection, use, retention, disclosure and disposal of personal information."[2]

The rights and obligations align directly with the basic legal provisions in GDPR, such as the right to access or the obligation to assign a Data Protection Officer.

But this is only a part of it. As the public becomes increasingly aware of their rights pertaining to privacy, the expectation of the individual will inevitably increase. This will in turn make it more important for organizations to focus not only on fulfilling legal obligations, but also on building a trust experience.

Part of this will develop as the legal obligations are met, such as giving easy access (individual participation principle) and easy to understand information (openness principle) to data subjects. This means you can no longer hide away privacy notices, and you must use a clear and plain language.

On a more philosophical or anthroposophical level, this is about creating trust among the societal actors: the individual, the organization and the government.

The Privacy Trinity

The three cornerstones of what we call the Privacy Trinity create the necessary trust among the societal players when it comes to privacy. The three cornerstones are:

- Rights of the data subject.

- Obligations of organizations.

- Enforcement of government authorities.

---

2 American Institute of Certified Public Accountants, Inc. and Canadian Institute of Chartered Accountants (2009). Generally Accepted Privacy Principles, CPA and CA Practitioner Version, April 2009, p.4.

Figure 13. The Privacy Trinity

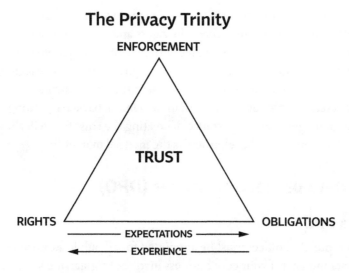

Rights of the data subject

The individual is represented by the data subject. All data subjects have expectations about how a data controller handles the personal data entrusted to it. The expectations will differ depending on a range of factors, from the type of data to the potential benefits of sharing it. Regardless of how good a privacy practice is on paper, it must still be manifested in the experience. Furthermore, the individual must also trust that the authorities will interfere and take action against data controllers that do not meet the appropriate privacy standard and thus are not fit custodians.

Obligations of organizations

The organization is in this context represented by the data controllers (to some extent also data processors) and, as such, must show they are a trustworthy custodian of personal data in order to keep the trust of the data subjects. But being a trustworthy custodian of personal data in the modern society means going beyond a tick-box compliance exercise. Instead, it should have the experience of the data subject in the center. This means taking the experience, values and trust into account. This is true regardless if the data subject is an employee, a customer or someone else. Trust is created by giving an experience that meet the expectations.

Enforcement of government authorities

The government is represented by the data protection authority (DPA). The DPA has the power to enforce the rights and obligations and the responsibility to oversee compliance with regulatory requirements. This is something lawmakers have identified as a goal, with the new legislation stating that rapid technological development requires a "strong and more coherent data protection framework in the Union, backed by strong enforcement, given the importance of creating the trust that will allow the digital economy to develop across the internal market."[3]

The data protection officer (DPO)

Why a DPO?

A data protection officer must be appointed for all public authorities and in private industry if your core business involves "regular and systematic monitoring of data subjects on a large scale" or processing of sensitive data. Before you are panicked into the hasty recruitment of a DPO, you need to consider that under the GDPR, the DPO has specific rights in addition to responsibilities. You need to take extra care when recruiting your DPO, as the GDPR does not permit dismissal or penalizing of the DPO for performance of his/her duties. What's more, if your DPO reports a lack of care in the collection and processing of personal data in your organization, you must listen and act.

Controllers and processors should designate appropriate resources to ensure that the organization will satisfy the GDPR's aim of giving the DPO an important internal- and external-facing role. Furthermore, the organization should make sure the DPO has the proper education, experience and skill set to be able to monitor internal data protection compliance. The DPO should also be given the necessary tools to fulfil the GDPR's requirements and to be integrated in the business operations, some mentioned earlier in this book

The DPO must have access to the company's data processing personnel and operations; independence in the performance of their roles; and a direct reporting line to the company board. DPOs can insist on the allocation of company resources to fulfil their job functions and

_____
3 GDPR, Recital 7.

for professional development training. The DPO role may be combined with other roles so long is it does not create any conflicts of interest. How a "conflict of interest" is interpreted depends to some extent on the member state. In 2016 the Bavarian Data Protection Authority[4] penalized a company for having its IT manager act as DPO, and this was even before enactment of the GDPR.

More often than not, the role of DPO has just been dropped in someone's lap as a side job—probably an individual lacking the budget and resources required to actually fulfil the tasks of a DPO. And frankly, most DPOs have not been too bothered about this since they have had other duties as well. This didn't go unnoticed by the politicians in Brussels; thus the GDPR ensures that the DPO has a central rather than a peripheral role within an organization. In order to achieve that objective, it provides a specific description of what the DPO role entails as well as what qualifications the DPO should have. Under the GDPR, a DPO will have new obligations, as well as new rights. In order to be compliant with new requirements, organizations will need to either assess the current DPO role or decide if a DPO needs to be assigned. The latter is highly recommended even for organizations falling outside of the mandatory requirement.

The rules related to the DPO can be found in three extensive articles[5] outlining the appointment, role and tasks of the DPO. According to these articles, the main task of the DPO is to ensure the internal application of the provisions of the regulation in his or her organization.

Designation of the DPO

The obligation to appoint a DPO has been heavily discussed since the publication of the first draft of the GDPR. The member states' positions on the matter were diverse, much as they were when the Data Protection Directive was implemented. The final text of the GDPR concludes that the appointment of a DPO is mandatory if any of the following are true:

- The processing is carried out by a public authority or body, except for courts acting in their judicial capacity.

---

4 Global Compliance News (2016). Germany: Data Protection Officer must not have a conflict of interests. (last accessed 2 January 2017) https://globalcompliancenews. com/germany-data-protection-officer-conflict-of-interest-20161121/
5 GDPR Articles 37, 38 and 39.

- The core activities of the controller or the processor consist of processing operations which, by virtue of their nature, their scope and/or their purposes, require regular and systematic monitoring of data subjects on a large scale.

- The core activities of the controller or the processor consist of processing on a large scale of special categories of data and data relating to criminal convictions and offences.

As you probably see, the term "core activities" is not clearly defined. In the private sector, the core activities of a controller relate to its primary, rather than ancillary, activities. Here we must emphasize that an earlier draft of the GDPR limited mandatory DPO appointment to companies with more than 250 employees, but this did *not* survive the negotiations. The final version has no such restriction. Instead, the obligation has been linked to the notions of "core activity" and "large scale" processing of special categories of personal data. The vagueness of these terms leads to some amount of uncertainty when trying to establish if a company is obligated to designate a DPO or not. This has to some extent been clarified by the Article 29 Working Party (WP29).[6]

One important statement from the WP29 is that "all organizations carry out certain activities, for example, paying their employees or having standard IT support activities. These are necessary support functions for the organization's core activity or main business. Even though these activities are necessary or essential, they are usually considered ancillary functions rather than the core activity."[7]

The WP29 also provided some clarity on the concept of "large scale" processing of personal data. According to the WP29, the following factors should be considered when determining whether the processing is carried out on a large scale:[8]

- The number of data subjects concerned.

- The volume of data and/or the range of different data items being processed.

---

6 WP 243, Guidelines on Data Protection Officers ("DPOs"). Adopted on 13 December 2016, last Revised and Adopted on 5 April 2017.

7 WP 243, p.7.

8 WP 243, p.7. On the following page WP29 gives some examples of large scale processing.

- The duration, or permanence, of the data processing activity.

- The geographical extent of the processing activity.

A controller or processor *may* always designate a DPO, whether it is required to do so or not. When in doubt, it will probably be a good idea to do so. And the WP29 also recommends that unless it is obvious that an organization is not required to designate a DPO, it should document the internal analysis carried out to determine whether or not a DPO would be appointed, in order to be able to demonstrate that the relevant factors were properly taken into account.

Notably, member states can adopt national legislation that expands the mandatory appointment further than the regulation. This means that for a trans-European company it may be mandatory to appoint a DPO in some countries but not in others.

Picking the right person for the job

It is highly recommended to let the DPO take part in setting up the privacy program since its development will partly depend on the qualifications of the person you hire. Thus, hiring a DPO should probably be the first step in setting up a privacy program.

Another initial consideration is whether you should have one or more DPOs. According to the GDPR, a group of undertakings may appoint a single DPO, provided that the DPO is easily accessible from each establishment. As a consequence, the bigger the group, the more difficult it will be to meet this requirement. If the undertakings are situated in a number of different member states it will probably also be hard for one DPO to have in-depth knowledge of all local laws. This is even more true now that the WP29 has stated that "[h]e or she must be in a position to efficiently communicate with data subjects and cooperate with the supervisory authorities concerned. This also means that this communication must take place in the language or languages used by the supervisory authorities and the data subjects concerned."[9] We touched on this earlier in describing the internal privacy organization.

At some point you will initiate the hiring. Oddly enough, the GDPR actually regulates on what grounds you should evaluate your candidates. Thus, you are legally bound by some qualification requirements for the DPO position, which means you can't just pick anyone you want.

9 WP 243, p.10.

Consequently, if you don't have an internal candidate meeting the requirements, you will have to hire one (or take in a consultant).

When it comes to the actual legal requirements on the DPO, GDPR explicitly states that the DPO shall be designated on the basis of professional qualities and, in particular, expert knowledge of data protection law and practices.

The DPO should also have the ability to fulfil the tasks assigned by the regulation. In this way, the requirements encompass both skill set and personal characteristics. The DPO will have multiple roles serving, supporting and representing conflicting interests. It will be a balancing act, not easy, requiring—on top of technical skills—mental strength, stamina and perseverance, as well as consistency in thought and mind.

At this time, we should also recognize that there might very well be differences between a DPO, a chief privacy officer (CPO) and a privacy program manager. The GDPR *only* set out the requirements for the DPO. The DPO will probably be a person with a legal background. The same doesn't need to be true for the CPO or the privacy program manager, nor for those holding the wide range of new titles that have seen the light of day in recent years. (Just to give you some other examples: Global Privacy Officer; Chief Counsel Global Privacy; Data Privacy Officer; Group Privacy Manager; Global Privacy and Data Protection Officer; Compliance and Data Protection Officer; and Compliance Officer Data Protection.) It is almost impossible to understand what, if any, differences are between them. These persons may, in some cases, serve as DPO. As time goes by we can only hope the titles will become more standardized.

Organizational support to the DPO

Perhaps most importantly, the organization must ensure that the DPO is properly and in a timely manner involved in all issues which relate to the protection of personal data. Organizations will need to integrate the DPO into team structures and resource planning, as well as amend processes to involve the DPO. That is why we emphasized this before. And this is actually something the WP29 also emphasized in its guideline by stating: "It is crucial that the DPO is involved from the earliest stage possible in all issues relating to data protection."[10]

---

10 WP 243, p.13.

Furthermore, the organization should support the DPO in the performance of his or her tasks by providing resources necessary to carry out these tasks as well as access to personal data and processing operations. The DPO should also be given opportunities to maintain his or her expert knowledge. According to WP29, such support includes:

- Active support of the DPO's function by senior management.

- Sufficient time for the DPO to fulfil their duties.

- Adequate support in terms of financial resources, infrastructure (premises, facilities, equipment) and staff.

- Official communication of the designation of the DPO to all staff to ensure that their existence and function is known within the organization.

- Access to other departments such as Human Resources, legal, IT, security, etc. in order to receive support, input and information.

- Continuous training.

- Given the size and structure of the organization, it may be necessary to set up a DPO team (a DPO and his/her staff).

Independence

A key aspect of the role as DPO is the independence. It is stated in the regulation that the controller or processor shall make sure that the DPO does not receive any instructions regarding the exercise of his or her tasks. In this aspect, it resembles an internal audit. As previously mentioned, there is also a prohibition on dismissing or by other means penalizing the DPO for performing his or her tasks. This could be problematic if the DPO fulfils other tasks and duties outside the DPO role (as long as the controller or processor ensures that any such tasks and duties do not result in a conflict of interest[11]). But will both roles

---

11 According to WP29, as a rule of thumb, conflicting positions may include senior management positions (such as chief executive, chief operating, chief financial, chief medical officer, head of marketing department, head of Human Resources or head of IT departments) but also other roles lower down in the organizational structure if such positions or roles lead to the determination of purposes and means of processing. WP 243, p.15f.. One example of conflicting interest is the decision by the Bavarian State Commissioner for Data Protection ("BayLDA") fining a company for

be clearly delineated? Should every communication begin by stating if it is made in the DPO capacity or that of the other role? And what if the DPO performs poorly? Can the employer do nothing?

The WP29 has at least made it clear that "[t]he autonomy of DPOs does not, however, mean that they have decision-making powers extending beyond their tasks pursuant to Article 39."[12]

Reporting

The DPO shall report directly to the highest management level of the controller or processor. This means that if the DPO does his/her job and reports shortcomings or lack of compliance, the top management will not be able to say they didn't know about such issues. However, the GDPR does not state how reporting should be done, or with what frequency. This will, as with so many other aspects of the GDPR, depend on the organization and existing reporting schemes. Some sort of continuous reporting by the DPO will likely benefit the organization. It should be stated that the DPO is bound to secrecy or confidentiality concerning the performance of his or her tasks, in accordance with Union or member state law.

The DPO will also, at least to some extent, need a budget. Without a budget, the DPO could indirectly be controlled in the performance of his or her tasks, thus calling the DPO's independence into question.

DPO tasks

The GDPR states quite a few mandatory tasks for the DPO. What follows is not an exhaustive list and most DPOs will probably do a whole lot of other things. However, the mandatory tasks include:

- To inform and advise the controller or the processor and the employees who are processing personal data of their obligations pursuant to the GDPR and to other union or member state data protection provisions.

- To monitor compliance with the GDPR and member state data protection provisions, as well as compliance with the policies of the controller or the processor in relation to the protection of personal data.

---

appointing its IT manager as Data Protection Officer.
12 WP 243, p.14.

- To provide advice regarding the data protection impact assessment and monitor its performance.

- To cooperate with the supervisory authority.

- To act as the contact point for the supervisory authority on issues related to the processing of personal data.

The DPO shall, in the performance of his or her tasks, have due regard to the risk[13] associated with the processing operations, taking into account the nature, scope, context and purposes of the processing. DPOs will have to consider how they will demonstrate the effectiveness of the controls and processes they are monitoring. Different industries or types of processing will require different levels of scrutiny and oversight.

Is the DPO liable for non-compliance with the GDPR?

Infringements of the obligations of the controller or processor regarding the DPO may lead to a fine by a supervisory authority of up to 10,000,000 euros or up to two percent of the total worldwide annual turnover of the preceding financial year, whichever is higher.

So, is the DPO liable for non-compliance with the GDPR? No, the GDPR makes clear that it is the controller or processor that is required to ensure and to be able to demonstrate that the processing is performed in accordance with the regulation.

Positioning and scoping the privacy program

How, where to start?

> **The most natural project-scoping parameters are by business process.** If you have not documented these, it may be a good place to start, and you don't need GDPR experts to do this!

Up until the fall of 2017, "how and where to start" were probably the most common questions being asked by CxOs within the European Union pertaining to GDPR compliance. Toward the year end, another common question evolved: "What are we doing wrong and how can we fix it?"

---

13 We must reiterate that this relates to privacy risks, not corporate risks.

It all starts with the basic necessary knowledge, i.e., a view of personal data as it flows through each business process. You need an account of personal data attributes by business process. And you should have assigned owners to business functions across your organization; these are natural personal data owners.

If you have business process documents, you have a good foundation to move forward with scoping parameters for your privacy projects.

Common mistakes

Starting too big

The most common mistake is that the GDPR compliance effort is treated as a single large project. If this is the case, your undertaking will never end (unless you drown on the way).

General advice is:

- Cut this elephant into small bite-sized pieces, i.e., smaller projects.

- Get a budget and get sponsorship for each project.

- Keep all projects independent of each other, so that the failure of one project does not block progress of the whole privacy program initiative.

- Hire some top-notch project/program managers to do this right.

- Use Agile as your project method, because one of the main risks of privacy projects is scope creep, due to the amount of relationships and actors interwoven within each project.

Using IT/application spectacles

A good place to start is to get evidence of data processing activities, and how better to begin than creating an inventory of personal data? You might think this would be pretty straightforward, but in fact, it's not. Unfortunately, some organizations have discovered that the product that they have purchased is an "asset register" repackaged as a "data inventory register," which means that even if the organization has a good description of business processes across their organization, they will be immediately frustrated because the views provided by the product are IT/application-centric, providing no business process view. If the organization does not have any business process descriptions, they will be none the wiser until later in the journey when they need to actually work with the product. It might be even worse, the asset register might not support data flow, leaving you without data flow charts and working in application silos without seeing the whole picture.

Another variation is when the organization tasks consultants to do this work, and the consultant firm uses its own "product" that is application-centric. The client can be unwittingly locked into the product because the data is the wrong view, i.e., not a business-process view. This really doesn't make sense, after all personal data is moving between applications and systems from the moment of collection until destruction.

What should be assessed are privacy risks on personal data embedded in business processes, or if there are no business process descriptions, you can try to take personal data (and call them personal data assets) stored in each application or system. For example, if you have a school system that includes data collected for student registrations, course delivery and teacher salaries, you have at least three distinct business processes, maybe more if any of them contain sub-processes. Each of these will have personal data (data asset) collected within the process, and this is how these projects should be scoped, by each distinct data asset. The reason why is that each has different purposes, collection points and end points, hence the associated risks are potentially diverse.

Digging too deep

Another common mistake is going too deep into the details before getting a helicopter view. You may have a team cataloging the trees, but it takes an eternity before you get a complete view of the forest. This is a risk because it could be undocumented parts of the forest that harbor the largest risks.

For example, there are some really excellent personal data inventory tools on the market, but they are requesting so much detailed information that it is almost like a mini-PIA on every item of personal data. This is fine if your business model is not complex, but for a large complex organization this will take a long time to complete. Start by cataloging as little as possible, as required by law, and enough to surface personal data with high privacy risks easily.

Don't reinvent the wheel!

By now I think it is apparent that compliance with the GDPR will necessitate changes on at least two levels within an organization: culture (management) and structure (privacy program). This is true whether you already have a privacy program and awareness training in place or not. The GDPR is so much more far reaching than any privacy law we have seen before. Therefore, you will either have to establish a privacy program as described earlier or kick your existing program into higher gear.

So here you are. You either already know, or have by reading this book up to this point come to understand, that you have been tasked with creating a privacy program. Perhaps that was the reason you bought this book in the first place. And now you are scratching your head. Where do you start? Where is the "low-hanging fruit" that you can pick easily without too much effort? Some things you can fix without needing to create time-consuming business cases with long justifications on why one should spend money on this specific project. Where are the "no-brainers"?

Privacy requirements are all about implementation and you probably want to kick ass and start the privacy program you have been assigned to build. Probably, you have read a number of step-by-step guides beginning with data inventory and ending with Nirvana in 12 easy steps. Hopefully, you have realized this is mostly a way of consultants milking you for the next four to five years. What should you do? Should you follow their advice and initiate the creation of a monster? Will you ever have the resources and processes to keep such an data inventory up-to-date?

Building a privacy program from scratch is hard. But in fact, you will not need to reinvent the wheel, nor must you build a monster of a project.

Think scalability. Start small and think "Lego" so you do not get overwhelmed. Build for the future and tag along with colleagues from other departments as you go. Even if you have started a giant inventory project, you also want to start yet another inventory—namely, an inventory of what your organization is already doing regarding data protection. We call this: "Go Fish."

Figure 14. Go Fish

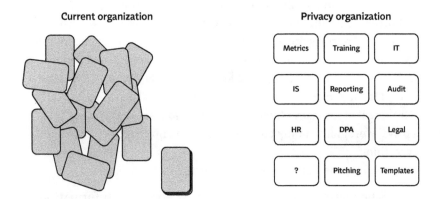

This is about creating order from chaos. Without a privacy framework within the organization, it might seem pointless to account for every little effort incorporated in a process, but putting all of those small bits together will hopefully show you a brighter picture than you first envisioned. And unlike many step-by-step guides, this method acknowledges that building a privacy program is not a one-off exercise. On the contrary, as stated in the Canadian document, "Getting Accountability Right with a Privacy Management Program":[14]

"A privacy program should never be considered a finished product; it requires ongoing assessment and revision to be effective and relevant. The building blocks must be monitored and assessed on a regular basis and be updated accordingly."

This is valid from the beginning, when you run around trying to map what your organization is already doing.

Going on a fishing expedition will also benefit another important characteristic of a successful privacy program: collaboration. Let us state this from the beginning: Collaboration is the key to success! Every department is equally important to reaching good privacy practice across an organization. All departments need to take part. One vital example comes from Northern Europe, where for a long period of time, only a handful of lawyers were interested in and working in the field of data protection. Most saw data protection as something for IT. We had a

14 "Getting accountability right with a Privacy Management Program," The Office of the Privacy Commissioner of Canada (OPC), and the Offices of the Information and Privacy Commissioners (OIPCs) of Alberta and British Columbia, p.2.

dichotomy where legal experts were nagging about compliance and tech people were going on about DDoS attacks and firewalls.

Fortunately, times have changed. Cooperation is the new black and going arm-in-arm is the way forward. Conflict between engineers and lawyers remains, to some extent, but as lawyers have learned about technology and tech people have learned about law, at least they have started talking. Here, it is worth reminding all legal privacy experts out there that no matter how much effort and resources you put into a privacy program, it only takes one mistaken line in the code to spoil everything.

Here are some examples of the departments to involve:

- Set up meetings with relevant persons working in **Information Security** and **Information Technology**. Among other things, they will be able to explain what kind of access you have as well as how the incident response works.

- **Human Resources** is involved in giving prospective employees and new hires information about organizational rights and obligations. In the best case, this already contains a privacy notice. If it does, you can review it and make sure it is giving information in a concise, transparent, intelligible and easily accessible form, and that the language is plain and clear. If it doesn't, you can help HR write it. HR is also likely to be in charge of training administration. Do not invent your own system, use the existing one to keep track of conducted trainings.

- **Communications** staff serve as a liaison with the public regarding an organization's work with data protection. Communications may also be responsible for the external web pages and Intranet. During the fishing expedition, you should look at all web pages. Most organizations today have a privacy notice, including information on the use of cookies. If this is the case, you should assess these according to GDPR and relevant local cookie legislation.[15]

- Larger organizations usually have an **Internal Audit** function. If your organization is in the financial sector, you are probably

---

15 The EU Commission is currently working on the so-called ePrivacy directive with the aim of turning this as well in to a regulation.

legally required to have this in place. Internal audit is used to assess compliance with legal requirements. In fact, it could be an internal audit report on data protection that actually caused the organization hire you in the first place. If not, you could ask the internal audit team to help you conduct an independent audit. This will ease your burden a lot and help you in your risk assessment and in planning forthcoming activities.

- The **Legal** department most likely handles contracts in one way or another. It could also be the owner of the contracts database. This database must be designed to support your needs as well. If you are lucky, you could find data processing agreements in the database.

Cut the beast into small bite-size pieces—you do not want your organization to suffer from indigestion!

If you have not yet documented your business processes, now is the time. What is great about this advice is that you do not need GDPR consultants to do this work, it's the Six Sigma[16] Black Belts you should bring in.

This documentation is not a privacy project, but it is necessary for the organization to reach operational efficiencies. So, you can push this up to the board, give them your priorities, and let them decide who takes this on. While they are busy getting this going, you can focus on scoping and organizing your privacy program. The goal with all GDPR projects should be to eventually evolve into a sustainable privacy program.

Pulling together a framework

Just as every organization has business functions, every organization has a "top-down" element, from where direction, vision, and mission are communicated along with rules concerning organizational ethics and best practices. From the top, one gets a privacy risk dashboard—a feed from the bottom-up component. An organization that does not have this will not grow beyond five or 10 employees. It is here you can position your privacy program. From the top down, you need to devise a privacy policy and ensure its incorporation into business operations as processes, procedures, and even work instructions.

---

16 https://en.wikipedia.org/wiki/Six_Sigma

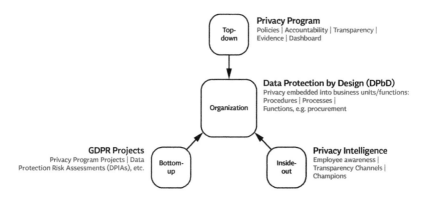

You can place your best program manager in charge of all privacy projects, and there can be many to start with. The entire privacy project organization is represented in the "bottom-up" component of the diagram above. Why is it called "bottom-up"? Often, budget for privacy projects is assigned by business functions (at least, this was the initial way). So, the idea was to get going with the budget allocated, and do your best to use outputs as a business case to "top-down." But this approach later evolved, and currently it gives an autonomous feel to the privacy program. It encourages organizations to keep projects manageable and in scope of departmental budgets. You can take this model and match to what fits your program. What is different about the "bottom-up" component is that it is forever changing. While a project is running, it will show up as a risk in the privacy dashboard (utilized from the top down) and upon successful completion it will disappear from "bottom up" and the risk mitigated by the project will be green in the privacy risk dashboard.

Then there is the "inside-out" component. Every organization has employees and needs to develop good communication and transparency in order to function smoothly. Today it is more complex than before, with every employee as a digital touchpoint of the organization, and thus potentially an ambassador for the brand.

Finally, there is the organization itself. In order to meet the requirements of the GDPR. it needs to be practicing Data Protection by Design and as a Default. Each of these framework components must to work in order to achieve this in practice.

Staffing and positioning of the Data Protection Office

A common question is how to organize your data protection office. It's always best to see what you have already and reuse, if possible. A good guideline is to look at how your information security or risk management programs are organized. If you are large entity, you will have direct reports and dotted-line reports. Identifying your competencies will help you decide who to bring in to complement your skillset. For example, if your strengths lie mainly with compliance and information security, it would be advisable to take in a legal "sidekick" to get you through the legal technicalities. If you have a legal counsel but are weak in compliance, then you need someone to fill that gap, and so on. As we mentioned, program/project management is basically driving the "bottom-up" component of your program. Finally, depending again on the size of your organization, and whether personal data is the core product of your business, e.g., finance and banking, you may consider bringing in a DPO as a direct report for each business function as shown in the diagram below.

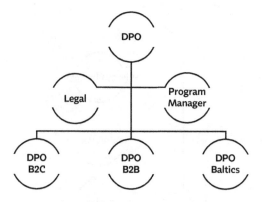

Clearly this diagram is missing critical roles (see below); the nature of your business, along with how your organization is currently structured, will influence where you place these roles.

What will be the same, across organizations, is the Privacy Champion role, filled by individuals that have become engaged in privacy issues. Check the section on employee engagement for more on this. Other positions, which could report directly into the business area if the organization is large with a dotted line into the privacy office, include:

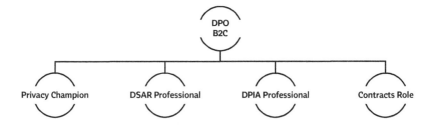

- **Data Subject Access Request (DSAR) Specialist**: Fulfils the rights of the data subject. This role is more pronounced in large organizations, and finance and banking in which personal data is a core product.

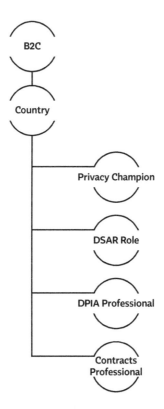

- **Data Protection Impact Assessment (DPIA) Professional**: At least one is required in most organizations, unless you contract this in.

- **Legal Contract role**: Deals with processor and agreements specific to GDPR compliance; this individual must have a legal degree.

> **A common misconception is that any employee should be able to conduct a DPIA**. This is the same as throwing a rookie on a complex project with unclear scope and large budget. **Treat this as a career choice for your top-notch Agile Scrum PM**, create a mentoring framework, and put them in your Privacy Hub.

The DPIA Professionals

The DPIA Professional

The main challenge with starting a privacy impact assessment is similar to that of any project: There is lots of noise, and you need to be able to discern the noise from what is relevant to the assessment. A clear in-scope/out-of-scope determination gets at this, but many seemingly competent individuals have a problem even at the scoping phase.

Moreover, you must have the capability to dive into details, without losing the view of the forest. If you dive too deep, too long, you will get lost in the noise. Individuals with great technical and/ or information security skills may not be the best choice for this type of project if they've never proved themselves as a proficient project manager. Basically, as with any project, if they get the scope wrong, the PIA will turn into an ugly beast! The DPIA professional is to conduct Data Protection Impact Assessments (DPIA) on personal data assets identified as high risk. The individual will need a mentor on their first two to three DPIAs. This is where it is important to have a mentoring program through the Privacy Hub, which we describe further in the chapter on Privacy Intelligence. If you have no DPIA experts in-house, best to bring in mentors from the outside until your DPIA professionals are feeling confident in their roles.

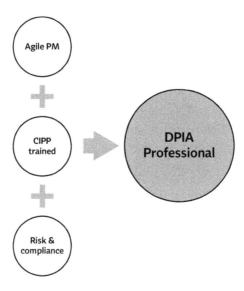

This position should be seen as a specialization, and a career choice within their personal development as it requires training. The ideal DPIA Professional fulfils the following criteria:

- Proven project manager.

- Competent in Agile techniques.

- Experience in creating data-flows.

- Comfortable with legal jargon; check www.iapp.com for privacy certifications (Certified Information Privacy Professional/EU, is the gold standard in EU data protection).

- Trained on a DPIA methodology.

- Experienced in managing risk.

- Experience in compliance projects.

- Can communicate effectively with all stakeholders.

The DPIA Mentor

The DPIA Mentor is experienced at conducting privacy risk assessments. They are a mentor to less experienced DPIA Professionals. The size of the organization helps to determine how long to initially use an external third party for this role. This role should be seen as a specialization beyond DPIA Professional, fulfilling the following criteria:

- DPIA Professional.

- Has completed roughly 10 DPIAs and demonstrated extreme competence.

- Is actively mentoring DPIA Professionals.

The DSAR Specialist

The Data Subject Access Request (DSAR) Specialist pertains to the rights of the data subject. This role handles requests from data subjects concerning their personal data.

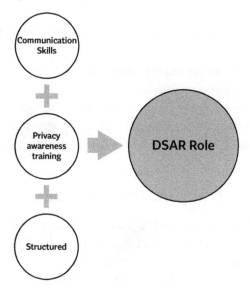

The DSAR role will need to ensure these things are in place:

- Business processes to process DSAR.

- Logging to evidence DSAR function.

- Metrics to measure effectiveness of DSAR function.

Certain factors will determine if the role needs to be full-time, part-time, or added onto existing roles spread over geographies.

Examples of influencing factors:

- If personal data is the core product of the business.

- The size of the organization.

- Its geographic reach, i.e., whether a DSAR Specialist would need to respond to each country in its own language.

It is assumed that processes are put in place to ensure that all requests are responded to within the GDPR's month timeframe.

The ideal candidate fits the following profile:

- Good communication skills, i.e., has previously worked in a client-facing role.

- Structured.

- Organized.

- Has completed privacy awareness training as detailed below.

Your employees are key to surfacing personal data that is being collected and processed but is not approved, i.e., not a part of an official business process and hence "invisible." This is personal data collection and **processing that is illegal** until it either stopped or cataloged in the personal data inventory, hence known and approved.

Employee privacy awareness training

Employees play a major role in the "invisible" personal data part of the personal data inventory project mentioned earlier. The problem is that they are likely unaware themselves that they could be collecting and processing personal data, because to start with they do not know what personal data is (or they think they do, but they are wrong). They may be unaware that just the act of storing personal data on a device is "processing." In short, every employee needs to be privacy-aware.

Employees are so sick of being spoon-fed yet another online compulsory organizational training, but it looks like there is no getting around it. Privacy awareness training is a must (the GDPR says so), and you need evidence that this training has been completed by every affected employee.

If you have a learning management system (LMS) in your organization, you will probably be looking at a SCORM-compliant e-Learning product to hook into it. If you do not, you will be looking for cloud-based products, which also need to provide you with evidence of learning.

Some approaches being taken today are:

- Sneaking a few slides on GDPR compliance into security e-Learning.

- GDPR awareness e-Learning.

- Make privacy personal with privacy e-Learning.

- "Nano-learning."[17]

- Brown Bag Lunch (BBL).

- Infotainment.

Sneaking a few slides on GDPR compliance into security e-Learning

This is quite common, but it is *not* a recommended approach. Justifications for taking this route to privacy awareness are: 1) privacy is a part of security compliance; 2) employees don't want another e-Learning; and 3) it's enough to show compliance.

However, this is not recommended, because:

- Privacy is *not* a subset of security.

- Employees will not change their behavior if privacy is treated as a part of security compliance.

- It is not enough just because it is a check-box approach (see table below).

The only way to do this is to empower every employee with an awareness that GDPR compliance, for your organization, is personal. An organization, after all, is a living ecosystem. The right to privacy touches every employee, not just in how they collect and process personal data in their work, but also in their personal life beyond work.

---

17 Nano-learning provides e-Learning content in "bite-size chunks," normally delivered as a series of over a period of time, with each learning activity not be longer than three to five minutes each.

GDPR awareness e-learning

It is *not* recommended to use the term "GDPR" in the employee-awareness training. Justifications for this approach are vague. It is quite likely that GDPR employee awareness is treated the same as Code of Business Ethics (COBE) or security training, so the same route is taken (e.g., same vendor for training material, who uses subject matter experts likely to be educated with a legal degree) for communicating to employees about their role in GDPR compliance.

Whether they are physically located within the EU or not is irrelevant, your organization will not succeed in getting full engagement of your employees in GDPR compliance by treating it purely as a business compliance requirement. This approach will merely add to the list of obligatory trainings that every employee must complete every year on top of a demanding work schedule.

Make privacy personal with privacy e-Learning

The seed of privacy is human rights. Every employee is a human being, so why not use that to get them engaged? If every employee realizes that privacy is about not just them, but also their families, their children and their friends, it gets personal. If they realize that the training will give them some great tools in their personal life, they may want to know more, and in turn become engaged, privacy-aware and caring employees.

A minimum duration of this approach to e-learning should include:

- What is personal data?

- What is processing?

- Why should I care?

In order to keep a privacy culture alive, over time you will need to complement this training with some nano-learning.

Nano-learning

The fact is, as interesting as a learning experience may have been, we will eventually forget its content unless we are exposed to the concepts in our daily work and or personal lives. Nano-learning is a great way to keep employees engaged about privacy.

Nano-learning sessions are normally between three to five minutes long. *It is* not *advised to use this learning approach in isolation, but as a complement* to your basic privacy awareness e-Learning activity. An effective approach is to link privacy issues with current events such as news stories about personal data that has been stolen or lost.

Table 7. Example of a privacy nano-learning activity

Learning activity	Quiz
Problem definition: • Yahoo lost personal data. • Two years later there was significant media coverage	1. What did they do wrong? 2. Do you think Yahoo suffered any financial loss from its personal data loss? 3. What would you have done differently in their shoes?

Brown Bag Lunch (BBL)

An American tradition that is received well by all. It's all about sharing knowledge, and there's a free lunch! You can invite a high-profile privacy speaker. Invite all employees to listen to the person while serving lunch.

Infotainment

The high-end of awareness is making infotainment. During the last couple of years both data protection authorities and consumer organizations have made fun, short films about privacy issues.[18] The film could be up-loaded to the Intranet and shown in conjunction with conferences, etc. Note, it should be fun!

---

18 One good example being the 2014 film "If your shop assistant was an app" by Forbrugerrådet Tænk, https://www.youtube.com/watch?v=xYZtHIPktQg

Learning Activity

For discussion in groups.

#	The Privacy Program
1	Jon White, head of legal, will serve as DPO to roll out the privacy program across SkinProds Online AG. What skills does he need in his team?
2	Twelve months down the road, Jon has realized that each business unit is "doing its own thing," especially in Finland, Norway and Denmark. There seems to be a lack of direction and a general panic, even though they have been working hard to collect evidence of data processing activities across all operational systems. He brought in IT experts to help. What could he be doing wrong?
3	Some confusion has occurred because the questionnaires sent out to ascertain where to find personal data has not been answered correctly. This has slowed down the data discovery exercise significantly. Personnel from the Privacy Office have been forced to go to the business units and deliver detailed instructions on how to answer the questionnaire. What do you think Jon should have done before sending out the questionnaire?

CHAPTER 5

GDPR Operational Efficiencies

GDPR as a change-management vehicle

The GDPR is a great excuse to do what should have been done before. Get your business processes documented and assure that your operations are aligned with industry best practices when it comes to processes, protection and dealing with emergencies. All those "nice-to-do" projects have suddenly surfaced on the board's radar.

Ecosystem

Controller, processor obligations

In order to succeed in the effort, every employee needs to know what is personal data and what is processing. Traditionally, it was only the legal department that really took an active part in data protection, but now—in every country and in every organization in the EU—it has become everyone's business. This demands investment in privacy awareness training, which needs to be repeated and included as part of the onboarding packet for every employee.

In order to succeed, privacy needs to be woven into all operations as stipulated by the requirement of Data Protection by Design as a Default. Finally, an organization needs to have evidence that they are doing all of this, and doing it right!

This is, in short, a change management project. It wouldn't be completely wrong if you are wondering how to deal with this. You may just start to realize that the resources needed to succeed in driving your GDPR program go beyond legal and compliance and IT. This section gives a taste of what could be a possible outcome when the culture of the organization changes.

Privacy culture and brand differentiation

Smart organizations view GDPR compliance as an opportunity to develop a new organizational culture, which can permeate the physical and virtual boundaries of an organization. It is a change management project, which can ultimately impact brand in a very positive way!

It is an awesome opportunity to differentiate in a market that has, over the last five to 10 years, woken up to the realization that to have a sense of social responsibility adds value to the business, brand and quality of employees they attract. The same can be said about compliance with GDPR, because its roots are in basic human rights.[1] This makes privacy personal and presents an opportunity to extend the value of your brand beyond a product or service and into the consciousness of every customer, partner and actor within your ecosystem.

How you become GDPR compliant will impact on a profound level your brand value, regardless of how you do it. For example, if you take the same approach as is has become the norm in information security compliance, i.e., do just enough to tick that little check box, it will impact the long-term success of your business. Your short-term financial gain

---

1 Defined by the Council of Europe in 1948.

on effort and engagement will be offset in the long term by business disruption and brand damage. By the year 2020, your marketing message will resonate as hollow and superficial compared to that of your competition, who have leveraged GDPR compliance to add a new dimension to the relationship they have with those in their ecosystem.

Weave privacy into the fabric of your organization so it evolves into its DNA. Data Protection by Design (DPbD) as a Default is a way of living and breathing privacy compliance. The GDPR stipulates that DPbD must be the default mode of operation in every organization.

Bridge the gap between the business, IT and legal

Data protection needs to be understood by all, starting at the board level and continuing to every operational aspect of your organization!

One of the biggest challenges facing organizations, regardless of size, is bridging the gap between the business, IT and legal departments, and it does not stop here. In order to make this work, you need a cross-disciplinary team and you need its members to be on the same page. This starts with getting "buy-in" from the board for those that need to make this work in practice. Skills and competencies needed to make this work: legal; compliance and audit; business process expertise; project/program management; technology/security/privacy architects and technicians; testing; communications; and HR.

The legal gap

"Legal" is made up of those legal geeks who eat "legalese" for breakfast every morning. The legal terminology rolls off their tongues with a finesse that triggers a blank stare in the recipient.

To set the scene, let us meet the board of the company ACME and John Doe, who works in the data protection office. John is a pretty smart legal guy. Nobody in the organization except John knows what privacy and data protection are, as defined in the GDPR.

Case study 1: The meeting of board - the legal gap

Meeting of board

CEO: Our data protection officer John Doe will be joining us in a few minutes to shed some light on how we need to tackle compliance with GDPR. Any questions?

CFO: Yes, I would like to know how we can measure our risk against the penalties for non-compliance.

CIO: I would like to know what technologies we need to buy.

CMO: Yes, and how about the marketing? Everyone is talking about "legitimate interest," and I have no idea what that is except that apparently we can't say it anymore.

CEO: Excellent, here he comes.

DPO enters the room confident; he has prepared well for this meeting. He's never been invited into the board room before, summoned by the CEO.

CEO: John, nice to have you here, you know we have been hearing a lot about the penalties for non-compliance with GDPR at 4 percent of annual turnover. Can you advise on what it means to our business?

DPO: Absolutely sir. I have prepared some slides and I am ready to take your questions. First slide gives a rundown of the six GDPR principles relating to the processing of personal data, with bullet points on what needs to be considered.

Okay, here we go, personal data shall be:

1. Processed lawfully, fairly and transparently.....

CEO: Hang on John, what does this mean to our business?

DPO: Well, it's very straightforward, if you don't do this, our business is not compliant with the GDPR. But let me continue, there's five to go....

CFO: Does it say how we measure risk in these principles?

DPO: No, but it does say later on that you need to conduct data protection impact assessments.

CFO: A-ha, OK, is this the same as a risk assessment?

DPO: Yes, except you're doing it on personal data.

CFO: Oh good, OK.

CIO: So, John, if I get a consultant in to do a risk assessment on our IT department and focus on personal data, that should work, right?

DPO: Absolutely, and you need to get evidence of your data processing activities too.

CIO: What is data processing?

DPO: Everything you do with personal data.

CIO: So, how do I do that?

DPO: You can buy a product.

CEO: I don't see why we need to buy any products we know where our personal data is: in HR, CRM...

CIO: Quite right, PII is pretty specific.

DPO: Personal data is more than PII.

CIO: In what way?

DPO: Here's the definition of personal data in the GDPR: "'Personal data' means any information relating to an identified or identifiable natural person ("data subject"); an identifiable natural person is one who can be identified, directly or indirectly, in particular by reference... "

CIO: You mean like through an IP address?

DPO: Yes, that's right. Look, let me continue and it will all become clear to you.

CEO: OK, John, go ahead.

DPO: "Personal data..., in particular by reference to an identifier such as a name, an identification number....

CIO: Is that not the same as PII?

DPO: Yes and no. It's more, it's any data linked directly or indirectly to the natural person, but let me continue.

"(b) personal data shall be collected for specified, explicit and legitimate purposes and not further processed in a manner incompatible with those ...."

CIO: What about breach notification within 72 hours, how does that work John?

DPO: You need to notify the Supervisory Authority within 72 hours of a personal data breach.

CIO: Yes, yes, but 72 hours, how?

DPO: Well, I really don't know how to do that...I'm a lawyer, not an IT expert.

CEO: John, thank you for taking the time to meet with us. I think we have enough now.

John realizes he's being dismissed.

DPO: OK, but I'm not finished...

CEO: It's OK John, we have a busy agenda. We'll call you again later.

John leaves the room.

CIO: I think I trust my team to take this GDPR compliance beyond legal.

CEO: Is everyone in agreement on this?

The board is in agreement.

That is the last time John gets invited to the board room and the CIO decides that IT will get the budget to do this work.

Is this an exaggeration? Yes, to some extent, but pieces of it will probably be true in most organizations. That is because there's a gap between legal (from either the data protection office or a consulting firm) and operations. This gap must be bridged to make GDPR compliance work.

The business, IT and security gap

In our scenario, there were some clear misunderstandings. The CIO felt on safe ground when risk assessment could be something he knew about already; he knew he had the competencies in his team to deal with this as well as breach notification, which clearly John had no idea about.

The problem was that the privacy risk assessment that John discussed was an apple and the risk assessment stated by the CIO was a pear. There was absolutely no understanding that the privacy risk assessment was something specific to personal data. However, the CIO thought he got enough understanding to hand it over to his IT guys. The IT compliance guys would have then treated privacy compliance the same as they treat information security compliance, using the ISO 27002 control framework, which has a few data protection tick-boxes under the compliance part.

Clearly this is going to go downhill, and will not be helped by any amount of so-called "GDPR product vendors" who say they'll solve all your GDPR woes with the touch of a magic button. Moreover, there is now a plethora of so-called "GDPR experts" practicing information security compliance, who, having done their data loss prevention and data classification projects, are ready to install themselves as chief advisor to the CxOs. In fact, they are able to speak in a language more understandable to CxOs, given their common understanding of business processes run over both business applications and IT systems.

A privacy language for all

Having a common organizational language to talk about GDPR compliance will make the journey easier, and possibly even transformative of organizational culture. If a common language had been adopted in the scenario above, there would not have been such a gap of understanding between John and the board.

The question is, how to get a common language that is understood by business, IT, security and legal? It needs to facilitate communication between legal and the rest of the organization. It needs get all parties engaged in the conversation. Those of you who have been engaged with change management programs will have worked out by now that tools used for engaging organizational change can be used here. It's also helpful to return to the common privacy language we covered in the section: A Privacy Language for All (only 8 principles)!

These principles have become the basic building blocks of privacy laws in every country worldwide, and they could effectively be considered the lowest common denominator in privacy globally.

Just to review the principles:

Table 8. OECD Guidelines - 8 privacy principles

OECD Principle	Description
Collection Limitation	Collect only what is needed for the purpose, and if necessary get consent.
Data Quality	This is not the integrity part of the information security CIA triad. We as individuals move house, change name, our personal data changes over time. It is the role of the controller to keep personal data up-to-date.
Purpose Specification	There must be a specific purpose for the collection of personal data. If there is no purpose you should not be collecting it!
Use Limitation	When your organization is using personal data, it is processing personal data; which includes the storage, sharing and destruction of it.
Security Safeguards	Whether you are a controller or processor, your organization must have sufficient security controls to secure personal data.
Openness	There should be a general policy of openness about developments, practices and policies with respect to personal data.

Individual Participation	The data subject has the right to know if the controller is collecting their personal data, what they are doing with it, etc.
Accountability	The controller must have the documented processes and procedures to evidence that these principles are being followed.

Let us return to John Doe, in the data protection office of company ACME. This time, all employees (including the board) have been properly trained (John too).

Case study 2: The meeting of board – bridge the gap

Meeting of board

CEO: Our data protection officer John Doe will be joining us in a few minutes to shed some light on how we need to tackle compliance with GDPR. Any questions?

CFO: Yes, I am wondering if he thinks some type of privacy risk dashboard aligned with OECD principles would be a good idea? If not, maybe he has other ideas for a visual view to help us assign budget by risk and priority.

CIO: I would like to know what technologies we need to buy.

CMO: Yes, and how about the marketing? Everyone is talking about "legitimate interest," and I have no idea what that is except that apparently we can't say it anymore.

CEO: Excellent, here he comes.

DPO enters the room confident; he has prepared well for this meeting. He's never been invited into the board room before, summoned by the CEO.

CEO: John, nice to have you here, you know we have been hearing a lot about the penalties for non-compliance with GDPR at 4 percent of annual turnover. Can you advise on what it means to our business?

DPO: Absolutely sir. I am ready to take your questions. First a slide that gives a rundown of the eight Privacy Principles that we are all familiar with.

CFO: John I am getting requests for budget to deal with GDPR compliance, is there any way we can visualize the risk to our business?

DPO: Yes, there is, we need to start by with getting evidence of our personal data processing activities, covered by the Accountability principle, number eight. I have discussed this with the department that has an overview of all approved business processes. My recommendation is that we start here because they have documented those business processes that have embedded personal data, and done a business impact assessment to determine what business applications and IT systems they run over.

CFO: Very good, is there anything more we should be thinking about?

DPO: Yes, it is likely that personal data is being collected and used in ways we are unaware of. I've been chatting to sales and know that we have sales executives who export CRM data onto their PCs to do a separate analysis. Some functionality is missing in the CRM system, so they are purely doing their jobs more effectively. However, this is of course not aligned with the Use Limitation principle. Hence, we need to get some awareness training out to all employees so they understand what is personal data and what is processing and can help mitigate this risk.

CFO: OK, John. Do you think you could conduct a gap on what needs to be done?

DPO: I will need some help to do this. I would not advise conducting a gap *per se*. I've been discussing this with our infosec team and I would suggest that we first do an "as-as" check, to see what we have before we trigger new projects. In parallel, we should start an inventory project on personal data—here, we might need to invest in a tool. We can start on some privacy risk assessments on HR processes in the meantime.

CIO: So, if we get in one of our external consultants in to do a risk assessment on our IT department and focus internally on HR personal data, that should work, right?

DPO: Not exactly. I talked to the head of IT; you've done a security risk assessment on IT operations, and they found that as far as the protection of data contained in IT systems, (i.e., Security Safeguards Principle) goes, it should be OK. However, when conducting a risk assessment on personal data, you need to bring in competencies that the subcontractor we presently use does not have. A privacy impact assessment must assess risk on personal data stored in business processes, such as HR payroll data, not by IT system.

CIO: Of course, thanks! One more question: what about breach notification within 72 hours, how does that work?

DPO: Well, we've already got some business processes we can reuse. For example, IT is using an incident management process that follows the ITIL process for service management. I recommend seeing if there is more we can reuse. We could start a project on this immediately; it is easy to scope because new skills are not required to do it. I recommend budget for this goes directly to the infosec group because they should already have a personal breach notification for our U.S. operations, which we can extend to our EU operations.

CMO: John, what's this about not being able to use "legitimate interest" in marketing. There seems to be significant confusion concerning this.

DPO: We should do a privacy impact assessment on all marketing activities because clearly we are using this now as a default, but this might not permitted under the GDPR.

CMO: So we can't use it at all?

DPO: Yes we can, but only under specific circumstances. In addition, there's a replacement for the existing ePrivacy Directive—due out by the end of this year or early 2019—called the ePrivacy Regulation, and this is something Marketing needs budget for, as it will impact that work. They can start by making sure they are following what is law today. I will help you with that.

CMO: OK, thanks John.

CEO: John, thank you for taking the time to meet with us. I think we have enough now.

John understands he's being dismissed. It is silent in the room some seconds after he has left. The CEO breaks the silence.

CEO: Are we all in agreement to hand over ownership and budget of GDPR compliance over to our DPO office, and the lead is John Doe?

The board is in agreement.

In this scenario, John has been talking to business process owners, IT and security before his meeting with the board. He is able to take out of those meetings useful contextual information because they have been using a common language.

The fact is, the data protection office will have a profound impact on how the organization collections and processes personal data. DPOs understand the rights of the data subject: basically, the data subject "owns" personal data, not the controller. This has a significant impact on how personal data is stored and accessed by authorized personnel. Look at the Individual Participation principle.

Specifically, the GDPR has a whole section pertaining to the Rights of the Data Subject which correlates directly with the Individual Participation principle. The data subject has stronger rights regarding personal data within the EU than is the case in any other country globally.

EU versus the rest of the world

The EU has the strongest privacy laws globally. It has a comprehensive approach to the protection of personal data, and the rights of the data subject. What this means is that the law applies to all personal data irrespective of industry or whether it is public or private sector.

The challenge that many organizations are having is that they are using "GDPR-speak" with their colleagues living outside of the EU; this can create a rift between legal departments. After all, every country has its own legal system and jurisdiction, and as far as they are concerned, only their laws and regulations are relevant until it comes to the transfer of personal data between jurisdictions. As far as GDPR compliance goes, transfer of personal data to a third country is possible only if specific rules are followed, which are covered under "International Transfer of Personal Data" (p.95). The thing is, if you are responsible for getting every division of your organization to privacy seriously, the GDPR way, you need to start at the level of your divisions—whether they are in Brazil, the U.S., or Russia—and bring them on board in a way that is transformative, rather than creating resistance.

This is where we return to the OECD Principles: the lowest common denominator in privacy; the building blocks of privacy laws in every country that has them. If you start at the lowest common denominator you can work your way up.

A good place to begin is with the privacy training you need to roll out across your global organization. This includes:

- Privacy awareness training that does not mention GDPR, but is in line with GDPR requirements.

- Engaging privacy champions. These individuals don't need to be experts in IT, law or security; your best champions are those who believe in privacy, and you can use that to get them engaged! Give them extra training covering the eight privacy principles and an intro to how privacy is handled within the European Union and other countries.

Openness and transparency as a core value

What comes first, the privacy notice or the internal privacy policy? It depends. Many organizations in the EU have an external facing notice but no internal privacy policy. If your organization has the luxury to implement both, then this section will give you the "icing on the cake." If your organization does not, then this section can help you establish privacy ethics that fit into your business.

What you are communicate to your customers and partners in your external-facing privacy notice, legal agreements, and other documents should mirror your internal privacy governance structure. In other words, you should practice what you preach.

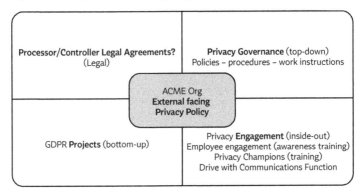

The privacy notice

The contents of your external-facing privacy notice should at a minimum contain the following:

- Identity and contact details of the data protection officer or privacy leader.

- Purpose and legal basis.

- Intention to transfer data.

- Legitimate interests.

- Retention period.

- Data subjects' rights.

- Statutory or contractual requirement.

- Automated decision-making.

> In a nutshell: **Whatever you do internally must reflect what you are communicating via external-facing privacy notices and legal agreements**, etc., when it pertains to personal data.

You will need your legal department to help you do this right. But let your information or marketing team write the actual words if you want it to be easy to understand, as the GDPR requires.

The privacy policy

When drafting the internal privacy policy, it is good to consider that it will need to be signed off on by the board. It should mirror your external-facing privacy notice, in that you should be doing what you say you are doing when it comes to the collection and processing of personal data.

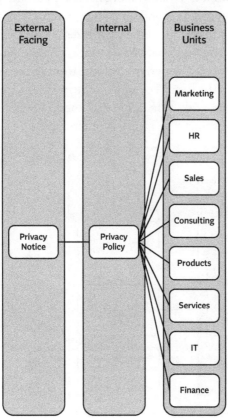

Try to keep it simple. Your internal privacy policy is an operational document. If it is complex and long, it means that:

- There will be a need to modify it more often, and each modification will need to go through the board for approval.

- Nobody will read or digest it unless forced to.

Up until now it has been common practice to have long, complex privacy policies. However, it may be smarter to slice it up and draft a high-level policy covering what privacy is about for your business on a strategic level and why it matters, along with high-level rules and a description of how it will slot into the organization's governance framework. It should be in a format from which sub-policies can be created to suit business functions and localizations at the country level.It should at a minimum dovetail with organization governance and provide hooks for each business unit and/or country to create their own steering documents. This will provide some strict rules without losing the autonomy that is important between business functions and geographies. You can use your privacy program structure to structure your policy framework. Just as the board will sign off the high-level policy, you will sign off sub-policies, and so-on. From here these should be transcribed into processes, procedures and work instructions at an operational level.

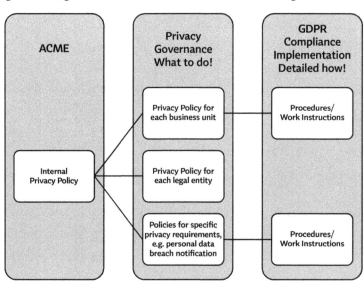

The framework in this section gives some tips on how you can make your privacy policies operational. Clearly every organization is different, but if you are following industry standards such as that provided by ITIL with IT Service Management (ITSM), you will recognize some of the terminology.

Privacy intelligence

In order to get data protection as the default operating mode for your operations, you need to treat this as a change management project. You need to facilitate a culture which permits transparent communications up, down and sideways, both internally and within your external ecosystem. This section is called "privacy intelligence" because it is about engaging the communications function into your privacy program.

The Privacy Hub

You could call this your privacy steering committee in a formal setting (or something else that fits the culture of your organization). Its purpose is to enhance the communications function pertaining to GDPR compliance across business functions and countries at all levels of the organization.

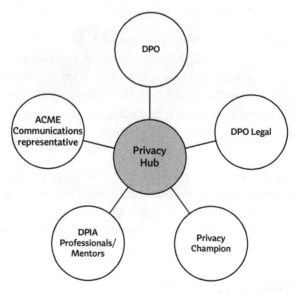

Examples of competencies and roles that could be included as members of the Privacy Hub are:

- DPO.

- Legal.

- Business functional DPOs.

- Privacy Champions.

- DPIA professionals and mentors.

- Communications representative.

Every employee is a "digital touchpoint" of your organization. Whatever they communicate in their digital interactions outside of the organization may not mirror communications over official channels. This is why a communications representative is included in the Hub. It is becoming common practice nowadays, when something negative happens to an organization, for media to ring employees directly and ask them about the incident. Moreover, every employee is an active communications channel from inside the organization to its external ecosystem. The consequences are that employees can (unwittingly or not) share information prematurely, or worse, information that contradicts the official story, over social media channels.

If your business suffers from a persona data breach, however well you manage this internally, and however well this is handled with the external messaging by your communications function, **your brand can be damaged by the communications over digital channels, such as Instagram, Facebook, LinkedIn, etc.**, unwittingly (or purposely) **by the employees** and also ex-employees.

If your organization loses personal data, your personal data breach notification process should be coordinated with the communications team, and dispatches by employees over their digital channels should mirror the official communications message. If not, your brand could be impacted adversely even if you are doing everything else correctly.

If you get the employee engagement part right, you could also have a flow upwards of transparency from your employees into your privacy program, i.e. privacy intelligence.

Engagement of Privacy Champions

The function of the Privacy Champion is to facilitate data protection communications up, down and sideways within the organization. As part of the Privacy Hub, they will be the informal news monger from the internal communications representative to all employees over formal and informal channels.

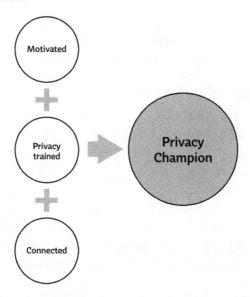

A Privacy Champion should ideally meet the following criteria: 1) highly motivated, 2) highly connected within the organization, 3) professionally respected and liked, 4) social, and 5) privacy trained.

Figure 15. Privacy Intelligence

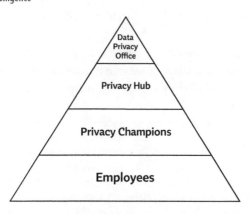

It is a great opportunity for employees who are motivated and want to do more than their job. They get extra training and recognition. These are the individuals that others will chat to about concerns on data protection that they may not be prepared to share via formal channels.

Compliance through privacy standards

After reading all this, you will be delighted to learn that there are some specific standards for privacy and other standards that include elements of privacy. Two of these will briefly be explained here.

The ISO 29100 Privacy Framework.

The ISO standard is rather Americanized in its wording, and not GDPR-specific at all. However, due to the fact that both the ISO 29100 standard[2] and the GDPR are essentially derived from the eight OECD Privacy Principles, there are significant commonalities. The ISO 29100 is a great tool for your technical team to use, just as the eight OECD principles are a great common privacy language for your organization.

As a processor, you may want to take a look at the ISO 27018[3] standard which is targeted at providers of web services which has packaged both privacy and security in a single standard.

British Standard 10012:2017 (BS 10012:2017)

On March 31, 2017, the British Standard Institution (BSI) published a new version of the BS 10012 Personal Information Management System (BS 10012:2017), enabling organizations to put in place, as part of the overall information governance infrastructure, a personal information management system (PIMS) that provides a framework for maintaining and improving compliance with the GDPR.

The system consists of seven areas or building elements for establishing a PIMS. Each area is then broken down into requirements and/or necessary steps in order to meet the standard. The seven areas are as follows:

---

2 The ISO 29000 standard can be downloaded for free at http://standards.iso.org/
3 ISO/IEC 27018:2014(en) Information technology — Security techniques — Code of practice for protection of personally identifiable information (PII) in public clouds acting as PII processors ISO/IEC 27018:2014 — Information technology — Security techniques — Code of practice for protection of Personally Identifiable Information (PII) in public clouds acting as PII processors

- Context of the organization.

- Leadership.

- Planning.

- Support.

- Operation.

- Performance evaluation.

- Improvement.

All requirements within each area appear in general terms and the individual organization will have to first assess whether or not the specific requirements apply to it or not. And, if it is applicable, how to implement it. The standard could be seen as a very structured way of describing a privacy program. As such, it could also be the foundation for a gap analysis about the maturity of the privacy management within an organization.

Living up to a standard based on the requirements and obligations of the GDPR, using BS 10012:2017, will help an organization show commitment to compliance with data protection requirements and best practices.

Privacy metrics

At some stage, most privacy programs will be challenged or at least you will have to defend your budget or justify why you want a bigger budget. CEOs and CFOs want easy understandable figures. What better way to do this than using metrics? This will also be very effective in demonstrating compliance and accountability.

What are privacy metrics?

Generally, metrics can be defined as quantifiable parameters or measures used for assessment regarding measurement, comparison or tracking of performance or production. For a long time, metrics have been used by management gurus or other business people to measure performance in economic terms, i.e., outcome compared to budget estimates. You might ask yourself how this relates to a privacy program. But as you remember, the GDPR does not only impose a lot of obligations on the actual processing, it also imposes an obligation on all organizations to be able to demonstrate compliance. Why not use classy diagrams and colored charts, perhaps in a PowerPoint presentation, to do just that? This will illustrate the shift from tick-box-compliance to accountability, with much more extensive requirements on documentation. The privacy program must also consist of privacy metrics documented over time. An investigation will not only find errors, it will also assess what you have done to mitigate errors from occuring in the first place, for example, by training the employees.

In addition, we can assure you it will not be long before all sorts of stakeholders will start to ask questions about the effectiveness of their privacy programs. Especially when the budget all of a sudden jumps up a couple hundred percentage points. Yes, we are referring to the top management, with the CEO and CFO as front figures. These stakeholders will not care much about the actual legal requirements and thus it will be much more useful to have a few slides with diagrams and graphs based on metrics to throw up on the screen, making the audience jump with excitement or hide with embarrassment. Regardless of the reaction, they will be assured that they hired the right person for the job: you.

Choosing metrics

What you should measure all depends on your organization and the maturity level you are at. Finding metrics that are relevant and beneficial for the organization is difficult, thus this will take time (and don't be afraid to change metrics over time). A commonly used acronym for metrics is SMART: Specific, Measurable, Achievable, Reliable and Timely.[4] Each metric must meet all of these requirements.

The right metrics should always answer anticipated questions from the stakeholders. It is all too easy to start with the question, "What can we measure?" rather than, "What should we measure?" Or: What questions from the stakeholders can we answer by using metrics?

Whenever choosing metrics, think about Ludwig Mies van der Rohe's phrase: "Less is more."[5] Simplicity is always preferable to complexity.

---

4 First introduced by Doran, G. T. in his article "There's a S.M.A.R.T. way to write management's goals and objectives." Management Review. AMA FORUM. 70 (11): 35–36, 1981.

5 Ludwig Mies van der Rohe was a German-American architect that lived between March 27, 1886 and August 17, 1969. He is considered one of the pioneers of

Don't hide the relevant metrics in a sea of irrelevant figures. For a fully mature privacy program, 10-20 metrics should be sufficient. In the beginning of a privacy program, maybe 5-10 metrics is enough. Choose wisely.

Next, we will give you a few examples of areas where metrics can be effective. We will also give some examples of metrics within each area and how you could use the metrics to show progress.

Training

Training and awareness among employees is at the center of a privacy program. Without awareness, a privacy program will always fail. Hence, it is most important to keep track of conducted trainings. An example is shown in graph below.

Figure 16. Metrics - number of employees conducted training

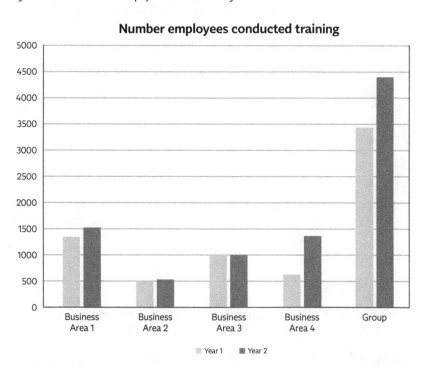

---

modernist architecture. His most famous work is probably the temporary German Pavilion for the Barcelona exposition in 1929. He is also famous for the quotation "God is in the details." Thus both his most famous quotations are just as important working with data protection as working with architecture.

What do you think happened after the first management meeting? Probably the BA4 manager made sure the figures looked much better the second time around on the next year's meeting.

Data subjects access requests

A dominating theme of the GDPR is to make it user-centric or put the individual in charge of his or her information. In order to achieve this, access requests have become more important. Our opinion is that an organization should measure different aspects of data subject access requests. Some examples could be: number of requests, time to reply on access requests, number of complaints following access requests, etc. See graph below.

Figure 17. Metrics – number of access requests and response time

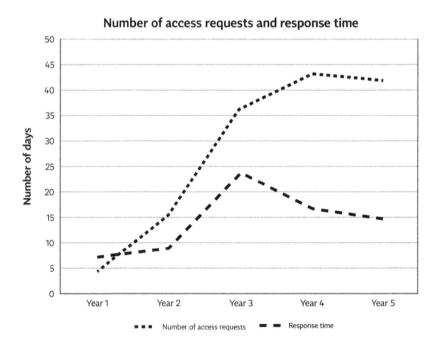

Types and number of personal data breaches

With the new requirement on notification of personal data breaches, it is a good idea to start to document and classify all breaches that occur.

Figure 18. Metrics - types and numbers of privacy breaches

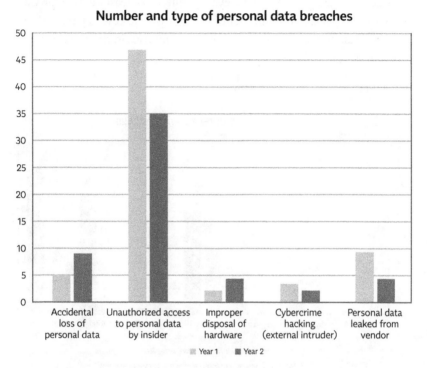

Number and type of personal data breaches

These kind of very easy-to-grasp graphics can be used both before prioritization and after mitigating activities have been taken. For instance, you would expect unauthorized internal access to decrease after a training initiative, otherwise the training hasn't had any effect and should be amended.

Access management

Just as under the EU directive on data protection, the GDPR states that only persons who need access to fulfil their job assignment should be granted access to personal data.[6] Despite this legal requirement, many organizations do not have an active access management system, meaning accesses are not granted and withdrawn in an appropriate way. From experience, we know it can be interesting to introduce a system wherein people automatically lose access to specific systems after a certain time of inactivity, for example, six months. Measuring the number of persons

---

6 This follows the security measures listed in Article 32.

with access to systems before and after introducing different forms of active access management can be eye-opening. Not least because privacy risks partly depend of the number of persons with access to personal data. An illustration of the outcome of using metrics in this regard is shown in the graph below.

Figure 19. Metrics - number of persons with access

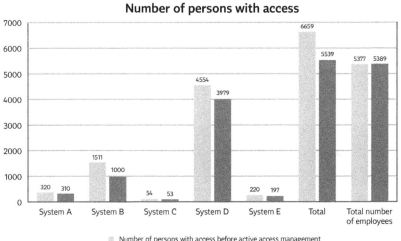

Gap GDPR and Privacy Program Maturity

Your privacy program probably consists of different areas. Each area most likely consists of a large number of actions. The more actions done, the merrier the maturity level. However you roll out your program (globally, business area by business area or department by department), the highest accountable management level will be interested in how the program is progressing. In the graph below, we have used maturity levels from 0 (shame on you) to 5 (fully mature). And for each area of the privacy program we have specified the maturity level over time, as well as the average for the whole program.

Figure 20. Metrics - privacy program maturity

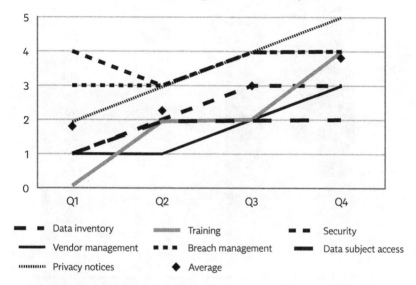

Privacy program maturity

Similar to privacy program maturity, you could also measure the progress of bridging gaps according to your GDPR gap analysis. This could also be used regarding the list of privacy risks and mitigating actions.

Figure 21. Metrics - gap analysis progress

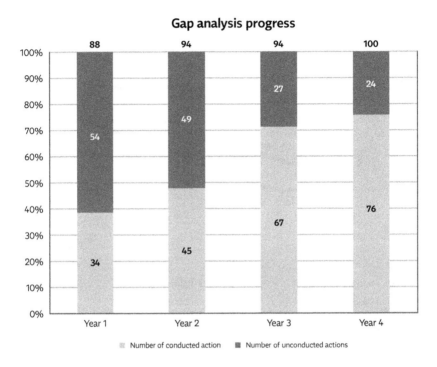

Learning Activity

For discussion in groups.

#	GDPR Operational Efficiencies
1	Learning Books AB has operations across 10 of the EU member states with an annual turnover of 100 million euros. The board has decided that the IT operations division will get the budget for GDPR compliance. They feel that Peter Jones, who is head of IT and a top-notch security guy, will do a great job. You have been brought into Learning Books as an external consultant. How can you help Peter make a success of this?
2	ACME Ltd. had a personal data breach and the "personal data breach notification" process went smoothly, following ITSM best practices. Moreover, the technologies were implemented and the employees are privacy aware. What went wrong?
3	The legal team has done a great job at creating an external privacy notice that is quite easy to read. An internal facing privacy policy has been created and translated into 10 different languages. However, 12 months have passed and feedback is coming that at an operational level the privacy policy is not practical, leading to the creation of regional policies to include national derogations, etc. Why has this happened? What are the risks? How can you solve this?

Appendices

Appendix A – GDPR Definitions (Article 4)[1]

(1) 'personal data' means any information relating to an identified or identifiable natural person ('data subject'); an identifiable natural person is one who can be identified, directly or indirectly, in particular by reference to an identifier such as a name, an identification number, location data, an online identifier or to one or more factors specific to the physical, physiological, genetic, mental, economic, cultural or social identity of that natural person;

(2) 'processing' means any operation or set of operations which is performed on personal data or on sets of personal data, whether or not by automated means, such as collection, recording, organization, structuring, storage, adaptation or alteration, retrieval, consultation, use, disclosure by transmission, dissemination or otherwise making available, alignment or combination, restriction, erasure or destruction;

(3) 'restriction of processing' means the marking of stored personal data with the aim of limiting their processing in the future;

(4) 'profiling' means any form of automated processing of personal data consisting of the use of personal data to evaluate certain personal aspects relating to a natural person, in particular to analyse or predict aspects concerning that natural person's performance at work, economic situation, health, personal preferences, interests, reliability, behavior, location or movements;

---

1 All GDPR extracts are © European Union, http://eur-lex.europa.eu/, 1998-2016

(5) 'pseudonymisation' means the processing of personal data in such a manner that the personal data can no longer be attributed to a specific data subject without the use of additional information, provided that such additional information is kept separately and is subject to technical and organizational measures to ensure that the personal data are not attributed to an identified or identifiable natural person;

(6) 'filing system' means any structured set of personal data which are accessible according to specific criteria, whether centralised, decentralised or dispersed on a functional or geographical basis;

(7) 'controller' means the natural or legal person, public authority, agency or other body which, alone or jointly with others, determines the purposes and means of the processing of personal data; where the purposes and means of such processing are determined by Union or Member State law, the controller or the specific criteria for its nomination may be provided for by Union or Member State law;

(8) 'processor' means a natural or legal person, public authority, agency or other body which processes personal data on behalf of the controller;

(9) 'recipient' means a natural or legal person, public authority, agency or another body, to which the personal data are disclosed, whether a third party or not. However, public authorities which may receive personal data in the framework of a particular inquiry in accordance with Union or Member State law shall not be regarded as recipients; the processing of those data by those public authorities shall be in compliance with the applicable data protection rules according to the purposes of the processing;

(10) 'third party' means a natural or legal person, public authority, agency or body other than the data subject, controller, processor and persons who, under the direct authority of the

controller or processor, are authorised to process personal data;

(11) 'consent' of the data subject means any freely given, specific, informed and unambiguous indication of the data subject's wishes by which he or she, by a statement or by a clear affirmative action, signifies agreement to the processing of personal data relating to him or her;

(12) 'personal data breach' means a breach of security leading to the accidental or unlawful destruction, loss, alteration, unauthorised disclosure of, or access to, personal data transmitted, stored or otherwise processed;

(13) 'genetic data' means personal data relating to the inherited or acquired genetic characteristics of a natural person which give unique information about the physiology or the health of that natural person and which result, in particular, from an analysis of a biological sample from the natural person in question;

(14) 'biometric data' means personal data resulting from specific technical processing relating to the physical, physiological or behavioral characteristics of a natural person, which allow or confirm the unique identification of that natural person, such as facial images or dactyloscopic data;

(15) 'data concerning health' means personal data related to the physical or mental health of a natural person, including the provision of health care services, which reveal information about his or her health status;

(16) 'main establishment' means:

a) as regards a controller with establishments in more than one Member State, the place of its central administration in the Union, unless the decisions on the purposes and means of the processing of personal data are taken in

another establishment of the controller in the Union
and the latter establishment has the power to have such
decisions implemented, in which case the establishment
having taken such decisions is to be considered to be the
main establishment;

b) as regards a processor with establishments in more
than one Member State, the place of its central
administration in the Union, or, if the processor has no
central administration in the Union, the establishment
of the processor in the Union where the main
processing activities in the context of the activities of an
establishment of the processor take place to the extent
that the processor is subject to specific obligations under
this Regulation;

(17) 'representative' means a natural or legal person established
in the Union who, designated by the controller or processor
in writing pursuant to Article 27, represents the controller or
processor with regard to their respective obligations under
this Regulation;

(18) 'enterprise' means a natural or legal person engaged in an
economic activity, irrespective of its legal form, including
partnerships or associations regularly engaged in an economic
activity;

(19) 'group of undertakings' means a controlling undertaking and
its controlled undertakings;

(20) 'binding corporate rules' means personal data protection
policies which are adhered to by a controller or processor
established on the territory of a Member State for transfers
or a set of transfers of personal data to a controller or
processor in one or more third countries within a group
of undertakings, or group of enterprises engaged in a joint
economic activity;

(21) 'supervisory authority' means an independent public authority which is established by a Member State pursuant to Article 51;

(22) 'supervisory authority concerned' means a supervisory authority which is concerned by the processing of personal data because:

a) the controller or processor is established on the territory of the Member State of that supervisory authority;

b) data subjects residing in the Member State of that supervisory authority are substantially affected or likely to be substantially affected by the processing; or

c) a complaint has been lodged with that supervisory authority;

(23) 'cross-border processing' means either:

a) processing of personal data which takes place in the context of the activities of establishments in more than one Member State of a controller or processor in the Union where the controller or processor is established in more than one Member State; or

b) processing of personal data which takes place in the context of the activities of a single establishment of a controller or processor in the Union but which substantially affects or is likely to substantially affect data subjects in more than one Member State.

(24) 'relevant and reasoned objection' means an objection as to whether there is an infringement of this Regulation or not, or whether the envisaged action in relation to the controller or processor complies with this Regulation, which clearly demonstrates the significance of the risks posed by the draft decision as regards the fundamental rights and freedoms of data subjects and, where applicable, the free flow of personal data within the Union;

(25)   'information society service' means a service as defined in point (b) of Article 1(1) of Directive (EU) 2015/1535 of the European Parliament and of the Council;

(26)   'international organization' means an organization and its subordinate bodies governed by public international law, or any other body which is set up by, or on the basis of, an agreement between two or more countries.

Appendix B – More on Consent

The legal entity, i.e., organization, whether a public authority or private enterprise, must log consent (legal basis for processing, Article 6(a)) and be prepared to show it as evidence to the data protection authority on request.

There are a number of different types of consent, these are discussed now.

Informed consent

A type of consent which we are all familiar with is when we sign with an old-fashioned pen a "consent" form, maybe concerning the use of our medical or other type of data in the name of research. Nowadays it is more common to find a hyperlink to the privacy notice. Within the form or hyperlink, will be an information giving us information on what we are consenting to. This makes the consent "informed." Informed consent is required in the GDPR. What this means in your business is that if you are requesting your customers share personal data on your website, you need to provide a link through to your privacy notice, so they are *informed* on what they are consenting to when they tick the box.

Under the GDPR, consent must in addition be "freely given," "specific," and "unambiguous."

Freely given consent

Consent from the data subject must be freely given. What this means is that the individual should in no way feel pressured to provide consent on the sharing of personal data. There cannot be an imbalance in the relationship between the controller and the data subject. For example, an employee (data subject) is not in an equal relationship with their employer (controller) in the context of their employment. Hence, it is not acceptable for the employer to use consent as the legal basis of processing of personal data shared by an employee. In this context the legal basis is normally Article 6(b), which refers to contract.

What's more, a controller may not make a service conditional upon consent, unless the processing is absolutely necessary for the service.

In the new regulation, it is not enough to place a tick-box for the data subject to agree to everything. You need to give them options for partial opt-ins. It is *not* an all-or-nothing approach. So, an example would be that a patient may agree to the collection of their personal data purely for the purpose of receiving a medical diagnosis, but *not* to be used for medical research. You cannot state that in order to get a diagnosis, they must share their personal and sensitive data for medical research. This creates an imbalance in the relationship of consent, which contradicts with *"freely given"* consent.

Unambiguous consent

So, what is *unambiguous* consent? Well, it is defined in the GDPR as similar to *implicit* consent but strengthened "by a statement or by a clear affirmative action." An example of this could be when the data subject ticks a box on a website or chooses a specific setting. Consent cannot be presumed purely with the act on continued use of the service.

Implicit consent is where by the mere act of continued use of a web service you are consenting to the collection of personal data.

Specific consent

Consent must be specific; it needs to be described precisely what the data subject is consenting to. The controller cannot request open-ended or blanket consent to cover the possibility of future processing.

Additional processing for archiving data in the public interest, statistical purposes, or scientific and historical research generally will be exempt from specific consent. However, there are strict rules on techniques that should be used for anonymization and pseudonymization of data in order to protect the rights of the data subject.

Opt-in versus opt-out

The default option in the collection of personal data under the GDPR is opt-in. What this means is that you cannot place a tick-box on a webpage or a form whereby your customers must tick the box to prevent you collecting their personal data. This is opt-out. The GDPR is very specific that the data subject, who could be your customer, must opt-in before you can collect anything!

It also provides that "the user's consent to processing may be expressed by using the appropriate settings of a browser or other application." However, in this case the browser's default settings must be to reject the placement of cookies, thereby requiring the user to actively opt-in to receiving cookies.

Withdrawal of consent

The rights of the data subject extend beyond the provision of consent to the withdrawal of consent. The GDPR gives data subjects the right to withdraw consent at any time, and it must be easy. In fact, the GDPR states that the withdrawal of consent should be as easy as giving consent. Once the data subject has withdrawn consent they have the right to have all their personal data collected erased, and it should no longer be used for processing, unless the controller can continue the processing on the basis of another legal ground.

Explicit consent

Explicit consent requires a signature, or an explicit action from the data subject, such as ticking a box before or upon the sharing of personal data. GDPR requires explicit consent for special categories of personal data. Sensitive data includes data "revealing racial or ethnic origin, political opinions, religious or philosophical beliefs, or trade-union membership, and the processing of genetic data, biometric data for the purpose of uniquely identifying a natural person, data concerning health or data concerning a natural person's sex life or sexual orientation."

Parental consent

GDPR requires *explicit* parental consent for processing children's personal data, when the child is under the age of 16 years old. Each EU member state has the option to reduce the minimum age to 13 years.

Controllers must make "reasonable efforts" to verify that a parent or guardian has provided the appropriate consent. Now as for what this means in practice, we can only look to the Children's Online Privacy Protection Act (COPPA)[1] in the U.S for guidance.

---

1 Federal Trade Commission. Children's Online Privacy Protection Rule ("COPPA"). https://www.ftc.gov/enforcement/rules/rulemaking-regulatory-reform-proceedings/childrens-onlinePrivacy-protection-rule (last accessed 7 January 2017)

Consent to profiling

Controllers need to obtain *explicit* consent in order to make decisions about the data subject using automated techniques. An example of this is profiling. This is most important when the effects of an automated technique, such as profiling, can impact on the rights of the data subject.